Advance Praise for *The Bravery Trick*

"As most Medal of Honor recipients report, their acts of bravery did not come from a conscious decision, but a compelling and selfless sense of what needed to be done in a moment. The social pressure to conform to popular thought and curb what we believe to be the right thing to do is around us all the time. Without diversity of thought, there is little hope for innovation and growth. Ed Evarts book will help provide food for thought to prepare you for a moment of opportunity—your moment of courage and bravery!"

—**Richard Boyatzis, PhD**, *Distinguished University Professor, Case Western Reserve University, Co-author of the international best seller,* Primal Leadership *and the new book* Helping People Change

$\cdot\ \cdot\ \cdot\ \cdot\ \cdot$

"We do not talk about bravery at work to the degree that we should, in an effort to help individuals and organizations grow. Ed Evarts's *The Bravery Trick* jumps right into the fray and helps us navigate these challenging waters effectively. Like dignity—a characteristic we all possess—bravery is equally important. Bravery helps others raise their self-awareness and find ways to move forward. Sometimes the best feedback comes from a colleague or friend who cares about your development–provide them the space to be brave with you.

—**Donna Hicks**, *Author of* Leading with Dignity *and Associate at the Weatherhead Center for International Affairs, Harvard University*

$\cdot\ \cdot\ \cdot\ \cdot\ \cdot$

"*The Bravery Trick* takes an experience that all of us encounter in our careers—avoiding saying something that might be hard to say or for the other person to hear—and provides some simple and easy steps to help you help others. Ed Evarts' use of client stories, podcast guest interviews, research, and insights help us untangle the behavior of bravery in ways that allow us to move forward. Not only is being brave to help others the right thing to do, it is also something we cannot avoid as our careers unfold."

—**Amy Edmondson**, *Author of* Right Kind of Wrong *and* The Fearless Organization*, Novartis Professor of Leadership and Management, Harvard University*

"Ed Evarts is a masterful courage encourager and The Bravery Trick offers a useful and practical approach for you to build the confidence and competence to speak up for what matters most."

—**Karin Hurt**, CEO, Let's Grow Leaders, and author Powerful Phrases for Dealing With Workplace Conflict

· · · · ·

"Ed Evarts has written the field guide for bravery at work – a universal topic that touches all of us. When we're not brave, we regret it. We let fear rule the day instead of summoning the courage to do what we know we should do to correct, protect, or add value in some way. Of course the fear is often justified because we often face rejection, retaliation, and repercussions, and there is no guarantee of a positive outcome. But if we're not brave there is an absolute guarantee that we will not have helped the situation. In this book, Ed takes an imminently practical approach to help us on both the skill and will sides of workforce bravery. His research and tools help us perform as agents rather than objects at those critical moments of truth that shape the future for all of us!"

—**Timothy R. Clark**, *CEO, LeaderFactor, author of* The 4 Stages of Psychological Safety, *host of* Culture By Design *podcast*

· · · · ·

"If you are seeking ways to say something that might be hard to say or you believe may be hard for someone else to hear, The Bravery Trick demonstrates key and actionable ways to make instant progress in being the brave contributor you want to be and to help your colleagues become better leaders."

—**Peter Bregman**, *CEO, Bregman Partners and author of* Leading With Emotional Courage

The Bravery Trick

Four Easy Ways to Say Hard Things

Ed Evarts

excellius
LEADERSHIP DEVELOPMENT

The Bravery Trick
Four Easy Ways to Say Hard Things

Published by

ed@excellius.com
www.Excellius.com
(617) 549-1391

Cover and Interior Design by
Robert Lanphear | Lanphear Design
lanpheardesign.com

Edited by
Lynne Heinzmann
lynneheinzmann.com

ISBN: 978-1-7345004-4-8

Table of Contents

Introduction

For two years, Radhika worked as a development manager for a San Diego pharmaceutical company, soliciting donations for important charities that her company supported. From day one, she loved her co-workers, her clients, and the donors, who often made contributions year after year. The only difficulty Radhika had with her job involved her immediate boss, SueEllen, who was habitually late for meetings or rescheduled them minutes before they were to begin. This caused work delays, missed deadlines, and extreme frustration for everyone on the team. Radhika often found herself thinking, "Why doesn't SueEllen respect our time? Does she think we have nothing better to do but sit around waiting for her to show up? Doesn't she care about us?" Although her boss's poor conduct was very disruptive, Radhika felt she needed to be a good team player, so, like everyone else on their team, she kept quiet and put up with SueEllen's bad behavior.

The situation came to a head for Radhika during a scheduled phone meeting with some very important annual donors. Everyone joined the call on time except for SueEllen, who showed up more than a half-hour late. She apologized and the call continued, but some of the donors seemed irritated by her behavior. Radhika felt embarrassed for herself, her organization, and even SueEllen.

Radhika wanted to do something to improve her work situation. She thought of speaking directly to SueEllen yet didn't know how to approach her or what to say. After all, SueEllen was her boss. Radhika considered asking someone else at the company for advice on how to help SueEllen, but she didn't know whom to talk to. No one had ever spoken publicly about such an act of bravery, and she wasn't sure how it would be received. And, most importantly to Radhika, she didn't want to be labeled a "troublemaker." In the end, Radhika—and her co-workers—did nothing, so SueEllen's behavior never changed. Shortly after the annual donor phone call, Radhika quit and found a position at another company.

Radhika's problem at work did not have to end this way. Instead, if the work environment at her company had supported bravery and she had been provided with the appropriate tools to handle the situation, she could have taken an active role in rectifying the problem. Radhika could have spoken to another organizational leader to obtain some advice on how to bravely move forward. With that support and information, she could have had a polite and brave conversation with SueEllen to make her aware of the impact of her behavior by providing SueEllen with real-life examples of how her behavior—whether intended or unintended—was having a negative effect on Radhika, their team, and the whole organization. If SueEllen had been receptive to this interaction, then they could have brainstormed ways SueEllen could behave differently to support a more productive work environment. Rather than becoming so frustrated with her work situation that she felt compelled to get another job, Radhika could have bravely dealt with the issues to improve her work environment, which would have allowed her to stay in a job she loved.

These types of situations requiring bravery occur all too often in our workplaces: Poor behavior goes unnoticed and unaddressed. Expressed concerns are minimized or ignored. Frustrations build to the point of negative actions.

When I look back on my career, I can recall several instances when I was not brave at work—when I did not say something that was hard to say because I worried that the receiver would not react positively to my comments. I reflect on these moments today, and almost always think of these events with regret. Why didn't I say something? Why didn't I ask for help from a colleague? How did I let this happen?

One example frequently comes to mind. John, a sales leader who had been previously terminated from our organization for low sales numbers rejoined our organization about three years later via an acquisition—he was employed by a company my company acquired.

As a human resources business partner, I was directed by my boss to immediately terminate John for a second time. From the moment I received this request, I was uncomfortable with it. Did we have to react so quickly? Were there other options available? Didn't everyone deserve a second chance? Yet, despite my concerns—and because I wanted to be seen as a good team player—I terminated John...again. I felt terrible. To make matters worse, when I told a co-worker what I had just done, he said, "Ed, I wish you had come to me. I would have found him another opportunity within the company." To this day, I regret my actions in this situation. Had I said something more purposefully to the decision-makers, I might have been able to help John succeed at our organization rather than lose his job for the second time.

To help us think about this thing called bravery, let's use this definition:

> ### Bravery:
> Saying something hard to say or difficult to hear to improve a situation and/or help a colleague grow and develop

This means that being brave at work is not about being judgmental, belittling others, or proving that you are right. It is about sharing with another colleague how you and others are experiencing him so he can be aware of this observation and take positive steps to improve his behavior.

Workplace bravery is not easy and even causes physical reactions in the person attempting it. When I had the termination conversation with John that I described above, my body tingled unpleasantly, and my heart felt as if it were about to explode. Jeff Haden, a columnist for *Inc. Magazine*, writes, "Just *thinking* about being brave triggers a flood of sensations. That's how we're built. The amygdala in our brains has a big job. It's in charge of our emotions and tasked with keeping us alive. When it senses risk, it can't help but jump in to save the day. You think focusing on being brave will pump you up, but since that makes your subconscious aware of the pain and danger, all it really does is cause a flood of stress hormones designed to stop you in your tracks. As your hands start to shake and your breathing grows shallow, you feel less and less confident—and your bravery abandons you in your time of need."[1] It's no wonder we often try to avoid situations requiring bravery.

But in today's work environments, bravery is vital. Recently, I chatted about the need for bravery in the workplace with a colleague of mine, Jayne Mattson, who is a career coach, a speaker, and the author of *You, You, Me, You: The Art of Talking to People, Networking and Building Relationships*. She said, "For years I watched or heard stories of younger employees and women who were treated disrespectfully or dismissively and never said anything about it. I would ask them if they wanted to be treated respectfully and almost all of these individuals said 'Yes, I do.' Yet these people lacked the courage, the words, and the assertiveness needed to be brave when someone treated them with disrespect." Standing up for yourself at work is one situation requiring bravery but, in fact, bravery is necessary during all crucial conversations that occur at work. In their bestselling book, *Crucial Conversations: Tools for Talking When Stakes are High*, authors Kerry Patterson, Joseph Grenny, Ron McMillan, and Al Switzer define crucial conversations as "a discussion between two or more people where (1) stakes are high, (2) opinions vary, and (3) emotions run strong."[2] Speaking up during such an encounter would certainly involve bravery.

While being brave may feel uncomfortable and is not easy, it is almost always worth the effort. Jim Detert, a University of Virginia Business Administration professor, and author of the book, *Choosing Courage: The Everyday Guide to Being Brave at Work*, says, "Choosing courage in key moments helps us build the legacy we want and avoid the regrets we don't want. Acts of courage at work can protect others, help solve problems and avert disasters, and lead to opportunities seized and to various forms of innovation and growth."[3] Kevin Callahan, co-founder and CEO of a national premium auto parts company, feels bravery is necessary to create effective business administrators. He says, "Bravery in the workplace is crucial to developing better leaders. It takes courage to be a leader. The instincts all leaders share to make calculated risks and reasoned judgments alike all take bravery to muster. Fostering a culture of courageousness in the workplace ensures everyone has those base instincts to survive crises and thrive daily with one another."[4] Bravery is the special ingredient that makes this all possible.

After I graduated from college, I worked for twenty-five years in the corporate world. And then for the past sixteen years, I've been a leadership coach, helping organizational leaders learn more effective ways to run their businesses. All of this experience has shown me the absolute necessity of bravery in the workplace. A few years ago, I began a twice-weekly podcast called *Be Brave at Work*© (available on Google, Apple, and Spotify), in which I interview various business leaders and ask them to relate their stories of successes and failures. And then, in preparation for writing this book, I conducted a survey of over 100 businesspeople, specifically focusing the questions on bravery in the workplace.

No matter where I obtained my information, though, the results were the same. In my bravery survey, ninety-six percent of respondents believed they could have been braver at work yet failed to do so. In my conversations with clients and podcast guests, I heard time and again how we are so busy and focused on our own performance, goals, and objectives, we fail to take the time and energy to bravely help others. And in my interactions with many different corporations, I observed that most of them do not espouse a culture that supports or rewards bravery in any way.

The Bravery Trick Model©

Based on this data, knowledge, and experience, I have developed a unique method called The Bravery Trick (TBT) Model© that provides four easy ways for you to say hard—but necessary—things in your workplace. This model works in both planned situations where you anticipate the need to have a brave conversation and unexpected situations where you need to be brave instantaneously. I wrote this book to share and explain the TBT Model© to you so that you can recognize and capitalize on the new opportunities for bravery that are waiting for you around the corner.

The TBT Model© is not like a magic or card trick. You are not trying to fool someone in any way. I use the word "trick" to refer to some easy steps you can take to say something hard to say or difficult for the other person to hear. In some ways, you need to trick your body and your mind—which naturally want you to follow the path of least resistance—into moving forward in ways that might feel hard yet are wildly beneficial.

In *The Bravery Trick*, we begin by examining how we are not brave at work. Then we look at the reasons behind this lack of bravery, followed by an examination of why bravery is necessary in a well-functioning workplace. After that, we explore the individual elements of the TBT Model©—Practice, Presence, Future-Focus, and Flexibility—in-depth and one at a time. We look at real-life examples of each of the four elements and then discuss how to foster an organizational culture of bravery, wherever you work.

Throughout *The Bravery Trick*, I share stories and examples from my podcast guests, results from the bravery survey, and observations from my work experiences to illustrate the ideas and suggestions presented. Also, I include actual survey participant responses so you can read about their workplace experiences and see how closely they parallel your own. Finally, I prompt you to create a plan with specific steps you can take to start making these necessary changes to be braver at work. Parts of this plan you will be able to put into action immediately and other parts will take practice, but regardless of where you are on this journey, by the time you finish reading *The Bravery Trick*, you will understand more about why we all avoid being brave at work and ways you can fix this problem.

There were many times in my life as a corporate employee and an independent consultant when I should have said something hard for me to say or difficult for a co-worker to hear, yet I didn't. Today, years later, I look back at these situations with regret because, knowing what I do now, I would have handled them much differently. Now, instead of avoiding those uncomfortable situations, I would work to improve them and try to help some co-workers, at the same time. I hope that by reading this book, you will learn how to disregard your tightened stomach, your sweaty hands, and your accelerated heartbeat long enough to succeed at being brave at work.

Let's get started.

CHAPTER NOTES
....

[1] bit.ly/3yX22rq

[2] amzn.to/3FGv5U3

[3] amzn.to/3lvudeb

[4] www.linkedin.com/pulse/why-bravery-workplace-matters-allellc?trk=pulse-article

QUOTES
from the Bravery Survey

"A colleague was being held unreasonably accountable by a manager who had his own shortcomings. I knew this was happening, and I never said anything about it."

. . .

"I was laid off from an organization for illegitimate reasons and I never did anything about it."

. . .

"I've passed up many opportunities to market my business more courageously because I feared rejection in the marketplace."

. . .

"I did not directly confront and talk with colleagues who were not supportive of a project I was leading, culminating in the project failing due to a lack of buy-in and executive support."

. . .

"I was a first-time manager leading a few individuals who were older and more experienced than me and they were often disrespectful of my leadership style. I regret that I let them get away with it."

. . .

"I did not come out as LGBTQ when, if I had done so, I could have helped support my LGBTQ clients and colleagues better."

CHAPTER ONE

We Are Not Brave at Work

"A lot of us would rather sit in the bubble of our intentions—
we intend to be good leaders, yet only twenty-three percent
of us feel our leaders are leading well. There is a huge gap
between what we intend as a leader and the feedback our
colleagues provide us of their experience."

– **Alain Hunkins,** *Keynote Speaker, Facilitator, Coach,*
Author, and Be Brave at Work© *Podcast Guest*
– Episodes 19 & 20

Like Radhika, the development manager mentioned in the Introduction, you probably have experienced moments at work where you could have behaved more bravely by saying something hard to say or hard for a co-worker to hear. But instead, you kept your mouth shut and did nothing. You allowed your queasy stomach, rapid breathing, and accelerated heartbeat to take the wheel and stop you in your tracks. Don't feel bad—we've all been there. Ralph Kilmann, CEO and Senior Consultant at Kilmann Diagnostics, co-created The Thomas-Kilmann Conflict Mode Instrument, which is designed to help leaders recognize and navigate through conflict in the workplace. As Dr. Kilmann says, "When I average the raw Thomas-Kilmann scores of groups, departments, and the whole organization, I usually find that *avoiding* is in the top twenty-five percent, suggesting that it is being used too much, while one or more of the assertive modes—*collaborating, competing,* and *compromising*— are in the lower portion of the profile, and thus being used too little."[1] Avoiding bravery is very common in our culture of conflict avoidance, where we are encouraged to ignore a colleague's bad behavior rather than create emotional waves by doing something about it.

Reviewing your career so far, recall a few of your missed opportunities to be brave. Some of them may have involved regularly scheduled events, like weekly project team meetings, while others may have been spontaneous experiences, such as a chance encounter with your CEO in an elevator. Maybe they were circumstances like these:

- Not providing your boss feedback that would have helped her be a better leader

- Disagreeing with an inaccurate assessment of your work but saying nothing about it

- Not raising your hand at a company meeting to ask an important question

- Failing to share ideas with your supervisor or other company leaders that could have benefited your organization

- Postponing a difficult decision that only got tougher to make as time passed

- Ignoring the feeling that something you were asked to do didn't feel right

In her article, "Top 10 Reasons You Don't Show Courage," facilitator, trainer, and coach Christi Barrett lists the following reasons business people are not brave:

- Some people won't like it
- It's more work
- It's too risky and I am not sure it will work out
- It's not the right time
- I don't want to seem pushy
- No one else is doing it
- No one will listen
- I'm okay with things as they are
- I'm comfortable taking little steps
- And, I'm afraid[2]

The list of missed opportunities for bravery is endless. Let's look at four specific examples of missed opportunities to be brave at work, based on the experiences of a few of my clients.

Failure to Provide Feedback to a Colleague

Caryn was an economic advisor at a consultant firm when Monica joined the firm in a similar capacity. To accomplish their department's objectives, Caryn had to work closely with Monica.

Very early in their work relationship, though, Caryn realized that Monica was not reliable. When Monica was supposed to provide supporting data, share notes from an interview, or simply give an update, she either didn't do it or failed to do it in a timely fashion. Caryn found this behavior extremely frustrating. She shared these frustrations with her husband and friends, none of whom worked at the firm, but she did not say anything about Monica to her boss or anyone else at work, as she was afraid others would think she was whining and would think less of her.

Instead, Caryn did what many of us do when working with an underperforming colleague; she changed her own behavior to compensate for Monica's substandard work. Caryn gave Monica false deadlines that provided additional time for Monica to finish her work or—if she failed to do it—for Caryn to complete the work for her. In addition, Caryn took on more of the workload herself, which increased the quality and timeliness of work being completed by their department but made her job much harder. Caryn never spoke with Monica or anyone else at the firm about these issues and frustrations, which made her personal job experience increasingly worse.

When she thinks back about this situation today, Caryn feels regret for not having the courage or the know-how to say something to Monica or others at the firm. Even though discussing the problem would have been difficult and might have been hard for Monica to hear, Caryn believes bravely speaking up about the situation would have benefited herself, her co-worker, and her organization.

ACTION

Recall a past example when you found the behavior of a boss, co-worker, or employee to be distracting or counter-productive, yet you did and said nothing to improve the situation. How do you feel today about your behavior in that situation?

Failure to Say Something During a Meeting

During Tobias's second year at law school, he was an intern at a large legal firm. His position afforded him the opportunity to sit in on strategy meetings involving complex litigation cases with many attorneys and other members of the firm. While Tobias had less experience than most of his colleagues, much of what he was learning in law school was fresh, current, and applicable to the cases discussed in those meetings. He often had ideas and suggestions that he felt could assist in their litigation.

Yet, Tobias did not speak up during those meetings. He was afraid that saying something unsolicited might feel intrusive to others, and he was unsure of how to engage in the conversation. He was intimidated by the capabilities of others at the meeting and feared that his ideas would seem junior and unimpressive. Also, he worried his contributions might prolong already jam-packed meeting agendas. And he feared his effort to contribute might irritate his boss and damage his chances of obtaining a favorable referral from him at the end of his internship. Regardless of the reason, Tobias rarely spoke up at the law firm's meetings. Today, Tobias feels regret for not finding a way to share his thoughts and ideas as he believes his suggestions would have been helpful.

ACTION

Think about a meeting you recently attended, when you had a thought or suggestion that would have been helpful, yet you didn't speak up. Upon reflection, do you wish you had said something?

Failure to Question Something You Are Uncomfortable Doing

Clarice's boss, Lewis, was smart, dedicated, and engaged. Clarice admired him and wanted to gain his respect. As a human resources leader for their firm, Clarice worked hard to ensure he saw her as a team player.

Each year, their large manufacturing company acquired a few smaller ones. After one acquisition, Lewis felt that Ruth, a leader from one of the acquired organizations, did not dress in a way that reflected her new company's culture and expectations. He asked Clarice to tell Ruth to dress more appropriately. Clarice had met Ruth several times and, while her dressing style was colorful, Clarice did not believe it negatively impacted her ability to get her job done or violated their organization's culture.

However, because Clarice wanted Lewis to see her as a get-it-done type of person, she did not tell him her opinion of Ruth's clothing. Instead, she met with Ruth and relayed her boss's harsh judgment. The conversation did not go well and soon after, Ruth resigned, stating as one of her reasons the feedback she had received regarding her clothing. To this day, Clarice thinks back on this event with regret for not challenging her boss's opinion and expectations.

In his article, "Team Project: Perceptions That Build Relationships at Work," writer and business management expert George Root III writes, "Creating an atmosphere of teamwork in the workplace requires the development of proper perceptions among staff members. When employees know what to expect of one another and the team as a unit, it becomes easier to create effective working bonds within the group."[3] We all like being a contributing member of a team and often believe doing what our boss asks us to do, even if we do not agree, is effective team membership.

ACTION

Remember a directive you received at work that made you feel uncomfortable, yet you did it anyway to be considered a team player. Today, how do you feel about your behavior in that situation?

Failure to Act in the Moment

While many opportunities for bravery occur at predictable times, during scheduled meetings or events, allowing you to prepare for them, sometimes a situation arises unexpectedly that warrants instant, on-the-spot bravery.

Phillippa was an employee at a pharmaceutical company that provided its employees with flavorful, healthy food in a large, centrally located cafeteria. Each employee selected her meal and then took it to one of four cashiers to pay for it. Since the cafeteria was so popular, there were often long lines at each of the check-out stations.

One afternoon, while Phillippa was waiting in line to pay for her lunch, another employee cut in front of her. Perhaps it was an innocent mistake. Although Phillippa was irritated by his rudeness, she held her tongue. Years later, she still asks herself, "Why didn't I say something to him? What was I afraid of?"

While this incident may seem insignificant, this type of interaction happens all the time—another person does a small thing that has a negative impact on you, yet you don't say anything about it. After all, being spontaneous is hard. As Saumya Kalia writes in her article, "It's Okay: To Not Be Spontaneous," "Spontaneous social activity burns through our energy reserves in double-quick time because of how much we have to think, react, and absorb when we're not mentally ready for it."[4] Hence, the biological requirements needed for showing spontaneity cause us to avoid being brave at the moment in the same way they stop us from doing acts of planned bravery.

ACTION
Think about a moment when another person did or said something that you should have immediately reacted to, yet you didn't. Today, when you reflect on the episode, do you feel remorse for not doing or saying something?

Occasions When You Were Not Brave at Work

As you read the above stories, chances are you remembered multiple examples of occasions when you were not brave at work. Perhaps you did not say something to a boss, peer, or colleague that would have helped her be more effective. Maybe you did not speak up at a meeting to share an idea that would have benefited the team. Or possibly you did not agree with a request for you to do something at work and yet you did it anyway. In all of these situations, you could have behaved more bravely but, for one reason or another, you didn't. And chances are that now you feel sorry about it.

This book will help you eliminate or reduce those feelings of regret by showing you how to respectfully and professionally be brave at work. By reading *The Bravery Trick* and adopting our bravery model, you will become a more effective leader and benefit your entire workplace.

CHAPTER NOTES
....
[1] https://mediate.com/the-avoiding-culture-in-organizations
[2] https://humanergy.com/overcome-the-top-10-reasons-you-dont-show-courage-at-work
[3] https://smallbusiness.chron.com/team-project-perceptions-build-work-relationships-10848.html
[4] https://theswaddle.com/its-okay-to-not-bespontaneous/#:~:text=Planning%20out%20days,%20knowing%20what,not%20mentally%20ready%20for%20it

QUOTES
from the Bravery Survey

"There was no support or coaching on the behaviors that would ensure people were not reprimanded for speaking up. When I spoke up, I was chastised."

. . .

"I hesitated putting forth a deeply held belief of mine about something I thought our company was doing wrong. Because I waited, when my thoughts did come out, they were unorganized and emotional, versus being level-headed, wise, and reasoned."

. . .

"I did not discipline an employee who was demonstrating bad behavior and who influenced others. The longer I waited, the harder it was to reverse."

. . .

"I did not tell a colleague how difficult it was to work with him and instead I tried to avoid him, which did not help us achieve what we wanted to achieve."

. . .

"Back in the 1990s, I was confronted by a co-worker and instead of sticking up for myself, I quit my job."

. . .

"I am such a people pleaser that I do not know how to say no, even though I end up taking on tasks that I do not have time for."

CHAPTER TWO

Why We Are Not Brave at Work

"We live in a knowledge world and most workers today are doing things that require their brains, their thoughts, and their ingenuity. When the majority of them do not feel they are part of their work, we are leaving value out."

– **Amy Edmondson**, *Professor of Leadership at Harvard University, Author, and* Be Brave at Work©
Podcast Guest – Episodes 28 & 29

The individuals mentioned earlier in this book—Radhika, Caryn, Tobias, Clarice, and Phillippa—all missed opportunities to be brave at work. They were faced with situations where respectful honesty would have been beneficial, yet they lacked the bravery and know-how to provide it, just as we all have done so many times. Why do we avoid being brave at work? Why don't we take situational or long-term steps needed to help our colleagues and, instead, run the other way?

In the nearly 300 conversations I have had so far with people from around the globe on my podcast, *Be Brave at Work©*, my guests have told me many different reasons they were not brave at work. Some said their inability or absence of bravery was due to the fear that being brave may have a negative impact on their jobs. Others said they did not feel they were the right person to say something potentially controversial yet helpful to a boss or colleague—that it wasn't their place to do so. Some felt too new in their roles to share their opinions, while others did not want to say something that might negatively impact positive relationships they had already established with bosses or colleagues.

Jim Detert, the professor, podcast guest, and author I mentioned earlier, writes, "There are four main kinds of risks to being brave at work: (1) economic/career risk, (2) social risk—being ostracized/socially alienated, (3) psychological risk—being embarrassed/falling on our face, and (4) physical risk—being accosted or assaulted in a customer-service environment. When you acknowledge all these fears associated with what people know or feel to be right, it's not surprising that many things are labeled courageous in the context of work. It's also deeply problematic because the failure to act in these circumstances leaves us individually and collectively in a much worse place."[1] In response to a question on my bravery survey—"Thinking about those moments when you could have been braver at work, which of these choices best describes your reason for not being so?"—sixty-four percent selected "Being afraid of the negative impact on my role and/or my job," or "Fear of negatively impacting relational energy (the energy associated with interpersonal interactions)." These are a few reasons for not speaking up at work, but there are many other ones as well. Let's look at some of the most significant reasons.

Lack of Bravery Lessons in Formal Education

Very few of us received any type of formal education on how to be brave at work. In my bravery survey, sixty-nine percent of participants said they never attended a single class in junior high school, high school, or college on how to demonstrate greater bravery in life or at work. This is a significant indicator of how our culture does not value or teach workplace bravery. We are so focused on *what* we want to become, we spend little time learning *how we operate* to become our best selves and to lead and help others most effectively. Let's clearly define the difference between those two concepts:

What we do = *The roles in which we engage to make a contribution*
Examples: *lawyer, fireperson, pharmaceutical engineer, manufacturing specialist, teacher, or nurse*
How we operate = *The behaviors and styles we implement to become*

our best selves and to connect, engage, motivate, and lead others
Examples: *conflict management, visioning, bravery, relationship building, change management, or influencing*

Most of my clients believe they would have greatly benefited from a high school or college class on how to operate in a workplace environment, specifically on how to be brave. When she was a student at Cornell University, Keira, a client of mine, noticed, yet did not take a class called "Courage, Humility, and Compassion." Since she was young and lacked work experience, she did not understand the value of these topics. Only years later did Keira realize such a class would have helped her be more skilled at saying hard things that may be difficult for others to hear.

Our Culture's Unrealistic View of Bravery

Our culture presents an unrealistic view of what it means to be brave. While there are historical figures for whom our recollections are accurate —Rosa Parks, Amelia Earhart, and Malala Yousafzai are examples of such individuals—our culture tends to applaud the magnificent, Hollywood types of bravery. We discount the smaller, everyday versions—the kind that would help us more successfully navigate the world of business. Here are some grandiose representations of bravery and how our culture presents them:

- **Washington Bravery:** These are big, bold statements that sometimes do not even feel real or are so heroic, we believe that only heroes could have done these things. Think of stories like these:
  - George Washington and his soldiers, crossing the frozen Delaware River in December 1776, with Washington bravely standing at the front of a boat, to unleash a surprise attack against Hessian forces in Trenton, New Jersey, or
  - King Leonidas and his 300 Spartans, confronting thousands of Persians in the battle at Thermopylae in 480 BC, or
  - The six marines who, on February 23, 1945, risked their

lives to raise the American flag at the Battle of Iwo Jima, creating an iconic moment (and photograph) that still impacts people today.

• **Entrepreneurial Bravery:** You may hear about an individual who started his/her own business in their garage by taking a second mortgage out on their home or maxing out a dozen credit cards. For example, Google, Apple, Amazon, Microsoft, Dell, The Walt Disney Company, Mattel, and Hewlett-Packard all began in the garage or basement of one of the organization's founders.[2] At first glance, these may seem like acts of bravery, but in fact, they may have been the result of desperation or limited options. You only hear these stories touted after the fact when the organization or idea proves to be successful.

• **Hollywood Bravery:** Millions of books and movies tell stories about bravery. Some of them are about true-life or realistic stories, such as books like *The Diary of a Young Girl* by Anne Frank and *The Red Badge of Courage* by Stephen Crane, and movies like Mel Gibson's *Braveheart* and Steven Spielberg's *Saving Private Ryan*. Some of the books and movies are obviously fictitious—so unrealistic or impossible because no one could ever be that brave. Think of the Star Wars, Mission: Impossible, or James Bond book series. These create the misperception that true bravery is bigger than life and can only be found on the written page or the movie screen.

• **Untrue Bravery:** We have all exaggerated a story or lied about an activity to make ourselves appear braver than we are. As kids, we did this to make ourselves seem more important, saying things like, "I ate at Matt Damon's house," or "My dad is in the CIA." In high school and college, we did this to impress our friends, saying, "I finished that book in two hours," or "I go out on dates all the time." As adults, we often see this type of bravery in politics and from folks looking for their fifteen minutes of fame. The Medal of Honor is the United States' highest military recognition. Since its inception in 1863, only about twenty individuals per year have been awarded this honor, so their accomplishments must be clear and confirmed.

Yet in 2011, Marine Corps Sergeant Dakota Meyer received the Medal of Honor, despite testimony from his military colleagues that his accomplishments were exaggerated and possibly did not merit this important recognition.[3] Untrue or exaggerated bravery exists everywhere and at all levels of visibility.

Our culture celebrates bravery, but it is often the unrealistic kinds represented in the examples above. We are given little information or instruction concerning the everyday type of bravery that would make a significant difference in our work lives.

Lack of Organizational Training and Acknowledgment

We cannot be brave at work if our organizations do not support our need to say what is hard to say or difficult for a colleague to hear. According to research conducted by Houston University Assistant Professor Priyanka Guchait and the University of Missouri Assistant Professor Seehonghee Cho, more than eighty percent of employees strive to work in healthy and supportive environments.[4] If your effort to be brave is not supported or feels professionally unhealthy, you are less likely to do it.

It is vital for organizations to invest in the following activities to recognize and support the importance of bravery at work:

- **Bravery Visioning and Valuing:** Most organizations have values, missions, and vision statements with goals and strategic objectives. They even have Management by Objectives (MBOs) to ensure the activities of employees support larger objectives. However, these same organizations rarely espouse any language or strategic objective focused on being brave at work to help everyone grow and increase effectiveness. As we mentioned earlier, organizations focus on *what* they are doing (i.e., manufacturing, profits, and calls per hour) more than *how* they are doing it (i.e., bravery and visioning). Imagine receiving a financial bonus or a letter of commendation whenever you behaved bravely or helped one of your colleagues be brave.

- **Bravery Training:** Because the strategic objective of bravery is not built into company values and statements, organizations do very little training on how to be brave at work or the benefits of doing so. In my bravery survey, seventy-seven percent of the respondents said they had never attended a workshop or a seminar on how to demonstrate greater bravery in life or at work. We do not educate individuals in our schools, nor do we train them in our workplaces on how to be brave at work. Think about how helpful it would be to attend a workshop on how to navigate conflict or how to have constructive conversations.

- **Bravery Role Modeling:** The strongest influence in your organization is the behavior of successful or more senior colleagues—role modeling. If leaders who demonstrate bravery or other difficult leadership skills are recognized and promoted, the likelihood of others patterning these behaviors will increase significantly. Yet, for many of the reasons we have already discussed, people are rarely directed or challenged to be brave at work, so the only ones exhibiting bravery are those who personally recognize its importance. This represents too few leaders in our organizations.

- **Bravery Recognition:** Organizations need to publicly recognize when individuals demonstrate bravery at work to promote bravery as an ideal. Why were they brave? How did they do it? What are the benefits of being brave? How is their colleague or the organization better because of this bravery? If moments of bravery were publicly recognized, other employees would seek this attention by copying the behavior, thus creating a culture of bravery.

- **Bravery Reward:** One way to ensure a desirable behavior is repeated is to reward the person for doing it. The reward could be financial bonuses, public recognition, organizational awards (i.e., Brave Employee of the Month), or extra time off with pay. If organizations rewarded their employees for bravery, workers would be more likely to repeat this behavior.

If organizations do not encourage, train, and reward individuals for demonstrating bravery, no one within the organization is going to risk being brave. Instead, the employees will invest their time and energy in the other areas of behavior for which they are recognized and rewarded. In their Harvard Business Review article, "Even Tiny Rewards Can Motivate People to Go the Extra Miles," authors Gerhard Furtmuller, Christian Garaus, and Wolfgang Guttel report that their research showed small rewards can help foster motivation and serve as a tool for behavioral change.[5] If companies want their employees to demonstrate more bravery, they must acknowledge and reward brave behavior.

Our Personal Reasons for Not Being Brave at Work

The most significant influencer in avoiding bravery at work is not education, culture, or training. It's our personal reasons for not being brave, which may include a lack of confidence, our past experiences with bravery, self-created fears, or our personality preferences. Let's look at these reasons in more detail.

Lack of Confidence

When asked why they hesitate to be brave at work, many of my clients and podcast guests mention a lack of confidence. They say things like this:

- I am too new in my role or at my organization. "I just started in this role. I want to ensure I have a great relationship with my boss without complicating our relationship so early on."

- I am too subordinate to the person to whom I should provide feedback. "I could never say something to her. She would be offended that someone three steps below her in the organization is providing this feedback."

- There may be other influences at play of which I am unaware. "How do I know what my boss is experiencing or why he made this decision? Maybe he is acting this way for a good reason."

This lack of confidence stops them in their tracks and prevents them from bravely acting or reacting to a situation.

Our Past Experiences with Bravery

Given our culture's attitudes about bravery, it is highly likely that you have had negative experiences when you've tried to bravely say what needed to be said or do what needed to be done. One client told me his family's household was so strict that voicing a contrary opinion or challenging a parent's decision was completely forbidden. Because he grew up in a world that discouraged being brave, he carried this behavior with him to his workplaces and never spoke up to his bosses either.

Our past experiences shape the way we respond in the future. If you were discouraged from behaving bravely in the past, you will be less likely to do so in new situations.

Self-Created Fears

In addition to all the external factors that negatively influence being brave at work, we also create internal obstacles that prevent us from saying what we believe we need to say or doing what we believe we need to do. My clients and podcast guests shared these self-created fears:

- I am under-skilled in providing candid feedback. "I have no idea what to say. I am worried that I may not say it correctly or that what I am attempting to say may come out wrong."

- I am afraid of the interaction with my colleagues. "I could not say anything like that to her. She will hate me, and I might as well call the unemployment office now and submit an application form."

- I am worried I will negatively alter my relationship with my boss. "I want to have a positive relationship with my boss and if I have to turn the other cheek every once in a while, and let unhelpful behaviors exist, it is worth it."

You may not have a factual basis for fears like these, yet they are very real to you and will affect the way you approach bravery in the workplace.

Our Personality Preferences

Personality preferences for the ways we choose to interact with the world also impact the way we behave at work: how we connect with others and how others experience us. Many self-assessment tools, such as the Myers-Briggs Type Indicator and the TypeCoach Verifier, can provide you with indications of choices you would make based on your personality type. Perhaps you have completed one of these assessments at your workplace or attended a workshop that provided you with information about your personality preferences and inclinations that can directly influence your interest and ability to be brave.

Rob Toomey, a personality preference expert, a *Be Brave at Work*© podcast guest (Episode 165), and founder of TypeCoach, believes personality preferences play a key role in how you demonstrate bravery at work. As Rob said to me, "When we ask someone to be brave at work, it should include whether the definition of brave is just a short list of universal behaviors or whether it requires asking someone to dig deep into themselves and, based on their personality type, undertake a departure from their comfort zone and face the fear that might come with a worthy goal."[6] He feels that identifying your personality preferences is imperative to managing your style when interacting with others. High self-awareness of how you operate is key to ensuring a reliable and consistent management style, while low self-awareness creates a highly erratic and unpredictable way of interacting with others. Knowing your personality preferences is a critical part of your journey to be brave at work.

Maslow's Hierarchy of Needs

In 1943, American psychologist Abraham Maslow wrote "A Theory of Human Motivation,' which explained some of his groundbreaking theories on developmental psychology. In this paper, Maslow identified a human hierarchy of needs in a pyramid-shaped graphic, which is pictured in Figure 2.1.

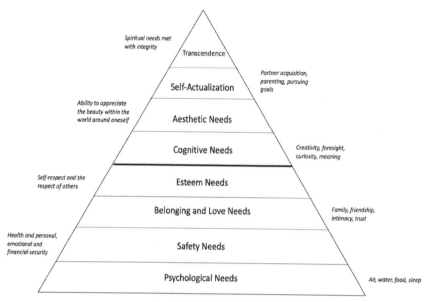

Figure 2.1[7]

At the base of the pyramid are our psychological needs such as air, water, food, and sleep, which, when combined with the second-level safety needs form our basic needs. The third level of the pyramid is occupied by our belongingness and love needs such as intimate relationships and friends, which join with the fourth-level esteem needs of prestige and self-respect for oneself and for others, which form our psychological needs, the lower half of the pyramid. Then the top of the pyramid is occupied by several need levels including our self-fulfillment needs of self-actualization—achieving one's full potential, including creative activities. Maslow believes for someone to reach his full potential in his work environment—the top level of the hierarchy of needs pyramid—he must first feel safe and secure—the second level of the pyramid. This may be another reason why you and your colleagues are not brave at work: any attempt you make to be brave and achieve your goals jeopardizes your more basic need for safety. Why would you risk being brave at work if the effort will potentially compromise so many of your essential needs identified in Maslow's pyramid?

In general, why should we bother sticking out our necks to be brave? Why not keep our heads down, do our work, and leave the bravery to the Arnold Schwarzenegger types? In the next chapter, we will review the reasons why being brave is instrumental to making us the best people and leaders we can be.

CHAPTER NOTES

1 https://www.forbes.com/sites/kimberlywhitler/2021/05/13/4-reasons-your-employees-are-afraid-to-be-brave-at-work/?sh=402f5f18487b

2 https://hackernoon.com/7-giant-businesses-that-started-in-garages-and-basements-cp6l36sy#

3 https://www.washingtonpost.com/world/national-security/marines-promoted-inflated-story-for-medal-of-honor-winner/2011/12/14/gIQAlhYwuO_story.html

4 https://www.tandfonline.com/doi/abs/10.1080/09585192.2010.483845

5 https://hbr.org/2016/06/even-tiny-rewards-can-motivate-people-to-go-the-extra-mile

6 https://www.typecoach.com/

7 https://www.simplypsychology.org/maslow.html

QUOTES
from the Bravery Survey

"I managed a person who was not demonstrating the same effort and drive as his co-workers, and I never said anything to him. To this day, my other hard-working co-workers are disappointed in how I handled this."

• • •

"I honored an unreasonable request by a client to expand an employee background investigation process even though this change added a lot of work to my team. I should have said 'No,' yet I did not, and I am regretful that I didn't."

• • •

"I was the senior leader of a team during a meeting when a higher-ranking employee demoralized a lower-level employee. I did not address this, and I regret this through today."

• • •

"I was reviewed unfairly regarding an incident and did not address this issue with my boss."

• • •

"I was going through a tough personal time at work and rather than be supportive and show empathy, my boss began picking on me and minimizing my future work opportunities. I ultimately decided to leave the company."

• • •

"I allowed myself to be harassed by another employee, which caused me to live in fear. I never did anything about it."

CHAPTER THREE

Reasons to Be Brave at Work

"When asked if I get nervous before a speech, I always say,
'Of course,' yet I know how to deal with that nervousness."

– Jim Cathcart, *Entrepreneur, Speaker, Author and*
Be Brave at Work© *Podcast Guest – Episodes 64 & 65*

In the Introduction, we discussed Radhika's relationship with her boss, SueEllen. If Radhika had been able to be brave at work, she might have constructively shared with SueEllen how her poor time management skills were having a negative impact on her colleagues and clients. Working together, they may have been able to identify some ways SueEllen could make positive changes to benefit herself and the whole department. And thus, Radhika could have helped SueEllen become a better leader.

There are many potential personal benefits to workplace bravery. As Kathy Caprino, an internationally recognized career and leadership coach, a *Be Brave at Work*© podcast guest (Episodes 93 & 94), and author of *The Most Powerful You: 7 Bravery-Boosting Paths to Career Bliss* writes, "It takes courage and strength to embrace new, confidence-building opportunities—to see ourselves as we really are, and to speak, ask, connect, serve, and heal courageously so we can become who we long to be."[1] This is especially true in the workplace.

In the Introduction, we defined workplace bravery as "saying something hard to say or difficult to hear to improve a situation and/or help a colleague grow and develop."

By being brave at work, you also promote personal development, advance your career, improve your leadership style, and provide role modeling for your colleagues and organization—all worthwhile accomplishments. In addition, being brave at work allows you to avoid the regret mentioned in many of the earlier examples, and promotes a feeling of dignity in yourself and others. Let's take a look at each of these important areas of potential growth.

Promote Personal Development

Most of us were raised to avoid being brave. We were not taught bravery during middle school, high school, or college, and our culture does not recognize or reward workplace bravery as much as it does grandiose Hollywood bravery. Therefore, by learning to be brave at work, we also are advancing our personal development.

Most experts agree that personal development is comprised of three areas of focus: spiritual, mental, and physical development. Being brave at work provides you with the opportunity to improve yourself in all of them.

Spiritual Development

Spiritual development involves connecting with yourself on a holistic level, developing as a person, and finding inner peace. It may be experienced through activities such as connecting with your faith community, volunteering to help others, practicing yoga, meditating, keeping a journal, spending time in nature, or focusing more on your hobbies. Effective spiritual development can also make you happier, which is critical to being brave at work. The website Aldohappy.com, which focuses on happiness inspiration, lists ten benefits of being happy in life including the following: improved physical health, increased resilience, and boosted productivity and success rates.[2] Spiritual growth is important to your development and growth because it helps you manage stress and build confidence in yourself and your abilities.

Judy, a successful consultant, did not feel she was accurately representing herself to her clients and felt some personal spiritual development was needed. She bravely changed her last name to one she felt better represented who she was. She also colored her hair a beautiful lilac shade, changed the way she communicated with colleagues by deliberately sharing leadership stories with them, and switched to doing management consulting work that utilized her true talents. All of Judy's brave changes provided her with spiritual development that allowed her to feel more like her authentic self, and thus gave her more confidence at work.

Mental Development

Mental development focuses on the advancement of how you think and learn. It also relates to the way your cognitive functions affect your behavior. It can take a variety of forms such as obtaining advanced degrees in your field or making a point to stay informed about current trends in your industry. None of these changes is easy and each one involves a concerted effort but, in the end, mental development leads to increased productivity at work. As former First Lady Michelle Obama said, "Through my education, I didn't just develop skills, I didn't just develop my ability to learn, I developed confidence."[3]

Savannah worked at a large payroll company yet longed to be an independent consultant. For years she did nothing to alter her work experience, feeling somewhat like a trapeze artist, worried that there would be no one to catch her should she fall. She finally embraced her courage and invested in some mental development. She extensively researched several different work opportunities and found the one that offered her the best chance for success. Then she quit her job, began her own business, and became a successful leadership coach. Her brave commitment to her mental development allowed her to obtain her dream job.

Physical Development

Physical development involves taking better care of your body so you can use it more effectively in productive ways. Your physical condition affects all other areas of personal growth and development, as a healthy body facilitates effective brain functioning. Dr. Kelly McGonical, the author of the book, *The Joy of Movement*, says, "When you exercise, it increases endorphins, dopamine, adrenaline, and endocannabinoid— these are all brain chemicals associated with feeling happy, feeling confident, feeling capable, feeling less anxiety and stress, and even less physical pain."[4] You can improve your physical development by eating nutritious meals, exercising regularly, and getting adequate sleep. When you feel better physically, you will find it easier to work more efficiently.

Krystal, a self-employed life coach, believed that her physical development had a direct impact on the energy and focus she provided to her clients, so she conscientiously slept eight hours a night, ate nutritious food, and regularly walked, jogged, and swam. As a bonus, her walking excursions took her across the globe where she made many valuable business connections, all possible through her brave commitment to her physical development.

Identifying Personal Development Goals

I have noticed that most people who are brave at work believe all changes start with themselves, so to achieve spiritual, mental, or physical personal development through bravery at work, you must first identify the aspects of yourself you would like to improve. Here are some activities to help you figure out your personal development goals:

- Take the TypeCoach online personality preference assessment (www.type-coach.com) to identify your personality characteristics, strengths, and areas of opportunity. Darnell, a partner in a successful consulting firm, engaged me to conduct a TypeCoach session with each member of his leadership team. Helping them identify their areas of strengths and opportunities and focusing on their communication styles greatly increased the likelihood that they would be brave at work with one another.

- Speak with brave colleagues, friends, or family members to find out how they operate the way they do. Ask them what they think about bravery, how they prepare themselves before an act of bravery, and how they feel afterward. The majority of my clients say they experience exhilaration when they show bravery.

- Honor bravery when you see or experience it. Take the time to speak to your colleague to acknowledge the brave moment you just witnessed. Ask her why she said what she said and what she hopes will be the result of her act of bravery. Speaking with a person who has demonstrated a moment of bravery will help you be better prepared when your opportunity arises.

- Hire a leadership coach or a life coach to help you build a leadership effectiveness plan focused on bravery that will help you make personal developments in the workplace. A *leadership coach* is focused on your professional life (i.e., career development, leadership growth, and navigating professional conflict) and can be a great partner to help you identify your professional leadership style, create a plan to overcome obstacles, and hold you accountable to your plan. A *life coach* is focused on your personal life (i.e., relationships, self-care, and exercise) and may be a good option if your focus on being brave is more personal. If you would like to know more about working with a leadership or life coach, visit the International Coach Federation at www.coachingfederation.org.

- Read books or articles that provide helpful information about being braver at work. Here are some of my favorites:

  - *Brave Talk* by Melody Stanford Martin (Broadleaf Books, 2020)

  - *Positively Energizing Leadership* by Kim Cameron (Berrett-Kohler, 2021)

  - *Helping People Change* by Richard Boyatzis, Melvin Smith, and Ellen Van Oosten (Harvard Business Review Press, 2019)

  - *Courage Goes to Work* by Bill Treasurer (Berrett-Kohler, 2008)

Remember that your overall objective is to learn about yourself, discover why you do things the way you do, and identify actionable steps you can take to make progress toward being brave at work. All of our personal development journeys are different. We each have unique strengths and areas of opportunities, goals and objectives, and varying amounts of time and energy. There is not one uniform answer that fits everyone. Your goal is to find the solution that works for you.

Advance Your Career

Another reason to be brave at work is because it will help you advance your career goals. Most of us want to feel we achieved a great career in which we collaborated well with our co-workers to make a difference in the lives of others, too. Being brave at work can help you accomplish your career goals in these three distinct ways: by more clearly defining your career direction, by improving your work relationships, and by allowing you to make a difference at your workplace.

Define Your Career Direction

Do you ever wish you had more time to carefully plan the future of your work life? Do you worry that you haven't been able to really think about who you are, where you are headed, and how you can get there? Hence, you may feel like only a passenger in your own career. You are puttering along, hoping that your work situation will improve, and you will be able to make a difference in the world. Instead of hoping, you should be bravely driving your career—ensuring it takes you in the direction you want to go. All change starts with you and, as the famous tennis player Arthur Ashe often said, "Start where you are. Use what you have. Do what you can."

Adjusting your career direction takes bravery. You may need to have a conversation with your boss, explore an opportunity outside of your current company, or investigate a career change. Raising your hand to talk about your own career development is often very hard to do.

Drew, an employee at an educational institution, contacted me because he was interested in switching from the passenger to the driver's seat of his career. He wanted to take on more responsibilities for projects at his school and believed to do that he must first positively influence his co-workers' perceptions of him. After I coached Drew through some brave conversations with his boss and other university leaders, they recognized his potential, and he was awarded leadership roles in projects. Through his workplace bravery, Drew was able to drive his career in the direction he wanted it to go.

ACTION

Have you spoken with your boss, a colleague, or a member of your human resource team about your professional career objectives? This conversation is not about work goals or objectives or client relations; it is strictly about you and your professional development. If you have had this type of conversation, what was the outcome? If you haven't had this type of conversation, find time soon to do so.

Later in this book, we will discuss The Bravery Trick Model© and demonstrate how positive change starts with you. Being proactive by bravely adjusting your career goals establishes you as a leader in your organization.

Improve Your Work Relationships

Another career advantage to being brave at work is that it will help you achieve and maintain strong relationships with your colleagues. And, conversely, you need those strong relationships to have opportunities to bravely help them and your organization. After all, if you approach a co-worker with a bravery-based comment, he is less likely to value your perspective if your relationship with him is weak or non-existent. Everyone you work with must know you well enough to trust that you are bravely sharing a perspective that might be hard to hear because you believe it will help them be better leaders. Deep and respectful relationships must be cultivated beforehand and demonstrating bravery with one another regularly is a great way to achieve these relationships.

ACTION

Think about the ten colleagues with whom you work the most. Do you have the type of relationship with each of them that would allow you to be brave when needed? If you don't, why not, and what can you do to improve those relationships?

Michael, the manager of a team of highly skilled professionals, hired me to improve the relationships between his team members. We first utilized TypeCoach to raise each member's awareness of his own proclivities and strengths, and then quickly moved to discussions and exercises that emphasized how each person's strengths could be optimized in the context of the team. By improving team relationships through brave discussions, the team members were able to work together more effectively and, in turn, many of them advanced their career opportunities.

Positively Affect Your Company

A third way being brave at work can benefit your career is that it gives you the chance to facilitate positive changes within your company. These changes will improve the work environment for you and your co-workers. Your boss and others in charge will notice you bravely taking a leadership role and they will remember you when it comes time for raises and promotions. In 1915, famed explorer Ernest Shackleton was in charge of a crew of twenty-seven men, trapped for six months in pack ice along the coast of Antarctica. Shackleton realized that waiting for the ice to thaw would cause tension among the expedition members that might escalate, resulting in dangerous consequences for their safety. So, he created what he called "mental medicine"—things for his men to do that would make them feel more productive, happier, and future-focused.[5] Due largely to Shackleton's efforts, he and his men survived this potentially torturous experience.

ACTION

While the challenges of your work experience may not equal Shackleton and his men's experience, think about ways bravery at work can advance your career by making a positive change in your work environment. What could you do differently than you are doing today?

Improve Your Leadership Style

If used effectively, being brave at work can help you improve your leadership style—the way you interact with others when you are guiding or managing them. Many organizations provide employees with tools they can use to identify their unique managerial gifts and how to use them to help others in their workplace. These same tools also show them how to adapt their leadership capabilities to best help specific co-workers. Effective leadership is a two-way street: you must bravely present your ideas in a manner others can comprehend and utilize them, plus you must bravely listen to others to hear where they are coming from and adjust your leadership style accordingly. Hence, when you think about how bravery at work affects your leadership style development, you must consider how you influence others *and* how others influence you, as well.

How Your Leadership Style Influences Others

Leadership style is a very complex concept to explain. VeryWellMind. com defines leadership style as "a leader's characteristic behaviors when directing, motivating, guiding, and managing groups of people. Great leaders can inspire political movements and social change. They can also motivate others to perform, create, and innovate."[6] Therefore, the goal of a great leader is to influence others to move in a particular direction. One prime tool of a great leader is bravery. They say what needs to be said and do what needs to be done to move others in a positive direction. Hence, if you want to be a great leader, you must demonstrate the ability to influence others by employing many skills, including bravery.

Fred Keller, the founder of Cascade Engineering, wanted to show that a for-profit business could also help address some of society's social ills—a strategy rarely espoused by for-profit organizations. Through a series of brave acts, failures, and persistence, all tied to his leadership style, Fred led his company to a novel employment strategy—hiring unemployed and under-trained local individuals—that benefitted everyone.[7] He used his leadership skills to influence the core attitudes and beliefs of his company.

ACTION

Think of a great boss or leader for whom bravery was one of her key characteristics. How did her bravery have a positive impact on you?

How Others Influence Your Leadership Style

Great leaders know that a successful leadership style must include more than directing, motivating, guiding, managing, and inspiring others. Leaders also must bravely allow themselves to be curious, listen, and accept the influences of others. In his seminal work, *The Seven Habits of Highly Effective People*, educator, author, and businessman, Stephen Covey, stresses that we should "seek first to understand, then to be understood."[8] His research shows that there is no better way to lead someone than to first understand her thoughts, perspectives, ideas, and beliefs. Once you know these critical data points, your ability to effectively direct that person is much greater.

Imagine if you were going to drive from New York City to San Diego in the days before GPS became popular. Prior to setting off on your trip, you would investigate the pros and cons of various routes. Then you would use this data to determine the best way to go. If you just hopped in the car and started driving west, who knows where you would end up and how long it would take you to get there? In the same way, you can lead someone much more effectively if you know information about her beforehand.

A leader is brave when she allows herself to be vulnerable and creates the opportunity for subordinates, peers, and bosses to positively influence her. Researcher, author, and speaker Brené Brown believes that vulnerability plays a key role in a leader's effectiveness. She says, "Vulnerability is not winning or losing. It's having the courage to show up when you can't control the outcome."[9] Great leaders recognize that being vulnerable is being brave at work, a critical element in the development of their leadership style.

ACTION

Think of a leader who demonstrated vulnerability to you. Was the outcome of the situation improved by his vulnerability?

Provide Role Modeling for Your Colleagues and Organization

As you build your leadership style by influencing others and allowing others to influence you, you are role-modeling brave behaviors that have a positive impact on your colleagues and your organization. In her article, "The Importance of Role Models," author and social observer Faye Syed writes, "Positive role models are essential at every stage in life: from navigating childhood to developing an identity in adolescent years, to chasing your dreams in adulthood. It is important to find people who inspire you to learn, grow, and push yourself to be the person you want to be."[10] And part of what makes those people effective role models is their use of bravery.

Your organization probably has a mission statement: a list of core values or a description of desired behaviors they hope will inspire their employees. But does that mission statement include anything about the need to be brave at work as a way to help others? According to my research, your answer is likely "No." All too often, the need for such validation is overlooked. Which makes it all the more important to role-model workplace bravery.

When someone role models being brave at work, he fosters an interest in bravery within the organization, which will get the attention of decision-makers. His behavior will help these administrators understand that being brave at work is a critical leadership behavior that must be indoctrinated into their company's culture. By doing so, he will promote the idea that being brave at work is something to be done by default, not ignored or avoided. As Bill Treasurer, the chief encouragement officer at Giant Leap Consulting and the author of the book, *Courage Goes to Work*, writes, "Avoiding interpersonal confrontation is a bigger inhibitor to team performance than misaligned goals, lack of planning, or misguided leadership."[11] If you want something to happen at work, you need to act as a role model and bravely put yourself out there.

ACTION

Consider ways to ensure that being brave is recognized as a necessary leadership style behavior in your workplace. What ways might you increase the visibility of bravery at your organization?

Avoid Regret

In the 2013 movie, *About Time*, a young man gains the ability to travel through time, which he uses to fix regretful moments from his past, such as the time he didn't kiss a young woman on New Year's Eve, the time he accidentally smothered a beautiful young woman's back with too much suntan lotion, or when he failed to save his sister from a devastating car crash. The central lesson of the film—spoiler alert—is that if you live each day to the best of your abilities, you will have no regrets and you'll never have to go back in time to fix things. Don't we all wish this were true for our lives? Unfortunately, we all have moments we regret, and our failure to be brave at key times creates some of the moments we regret the most. In my bravery survey, ninety-three percent of the respondents said they hadn't taken advantage of at least one opportunity to be brave at work and they regretted it.

In his book, *The Power of Regret*, Daniel Pink postulates that having regrets isn't always bad and, in fact, is a behavioral characteristic that makes us human. Pink states three benefits of regret: it can improve decisions, boost performance, and create deeper meanings.[12]

Regret can improve decisions since we learn from the past. For example, if you are a newly licensed plumber, you may regret charging too little for your services at first. Yet, as time goes by, you can use this information to adjust your rates to be more appropriately priced for your market. Your regret teaches you how to be a better businessperson.

And regret can boost performance, too. If you feel poorly about how you did something in the past, you might try harder to improve your performance in the future. Nathan Chen, the figure skater, had a disastrous performance at the 2018 Olympics, finishing fifth in an event he was favored to win. Nathan greatly regretted his performance, but instead of giving up, he worked harder than ever to learn from his mistakes, so that four years later he achieved his highest Olympic achievement—a gold medal at the 2022 Games. No one wants to continue making the same mistakes over and over again and regret can prompt you to avoid this.

And lastly, regret can deepen the meaning of our lives. In his book, Pink suggests that each of us review our lives, concentrating on our regrets. He writes, "Research has found that people who thought counterfactually about pivotal moments in their life experienced greater meaning than people who thought explicitly about the meaning of those events... Conducting a midlife review focused on regrets can prompt us to revise our life goals and aim to live afresh." Yet another positive effect of regrets.

Promote Dignity

Whenever you bravely share feedback with a colleague, it is important to frame the conversation around the question, "How do I help my colleague?" If your goal is to judge or belittle your colleague's behavior, that is not being brave at work. In fact, there is no place for this behavior in life or your workplace.

In her book, *Leading with Dignity*, Donna Hicks, author, associate professor at Harvard University, and a *Be Brave at Work*© podcast guest (Episodes 218 & 219), shares her insights about the importance of dignity in corporate environments. "Dignity is our inherent value and worth, vulnerable to being harmed and injured."[13] We are all born with dignity, we all have value and worth, and we all expect to be treated with dignity, regardless of the topic or situation.

This is why we must consider whether we are helping or hurting when we bravely say something that needs to be said or do something that needs to be done. No one wants to be judged or belittled by a colleague. It tarnishes his dignity. It becomes hurtful. In contrast, if you want to help him see something that perhaps he is not seeing on his own and you share this information with the intention of helping him, his dignity is respected, and he will appreciate your candor.

There are many, many reasons to be brave at work. It promotes your personal development, advances your career, improves your leadership style, provides positive role modeling for your co-workers, allows you to avoid regret, and promotes a sense of dignity in yourself and those you work with. No one can be brave at work all the time. Yet, by using some of the ideas from this book, you will learn to maximize your opportunities for bravery and minimize your regrets.

CHAPTER NOTES

....

[1] https://www.amazon.com/Most-Powerful-You-Bravery-Boosting-Career/ dp/1400217482/ref=sr_1_1?crid=30MPYLNPQS8BZ&keywords=kathy+- caprino&qid=1679252504&sprefix=kathy+caprino,aps,88&sr=8-1

[2] https://aldohappy.com/benefits-of-being-happy#:~:text=Happiness%20 Increases%20Your%20Resilience,better%20with%20anxiety%20and%20 depression.

[3] https://togetherband.org/blogs/news/michelle-obama-quotes#:~:tex- t=%27Through%20my%20education%2C%20I%20didn,%27

[4] https://www.thehabitista.com/health/12-exercise-and-mental-health- quotes-live-a-better-life/#:~:text=I%20feel%20better%20in%20my,It%20 makes%20everything%20better.&text=It%20doesn%27t%20really%20mat- ter,and%20the%20other%20way%20around.

[5] https://online.hbs.edu/blog/post/courageous-leaders

[6] https://www.verywellmind.com/leadership-styles-2795312

[7] https://hbr.org/2022/01/what-courageous-leaders-do-differently

[8] https://www.amazon.com/Habits-Highly-Effective-People-Power- ful/dp/1982137274/ref=sr_1_1?crid=16VRJXLCDXRET&key- words=seven+habits+of+highly+effective+people+by+stephen+cov- ey&qid=1679253097&sprefix=seven+habi,aps,93&sr=8-1

[9] https://www.amazon.com/Dare-Lead-Brave-Conversations-Hearts/ dp/0399592520/ref=sr_1_8?crid=3ASRZE9JJ0XZ8&key- words=brene+brown+books&qid=1679253228&sprefix=brene+brown+- books,aps,87&sr=8-8

[10] https://inkspire.org/post/the-importance-of-role-models/-MAiDs- DL728dR9ZnAXBq

[11] https://www.amazon.com/Courage-Goes-Work-Backbones-Performance/ dp/1523098562/ref=sr_1_4?crid=3NUIJQJGSQI0O&keywords=bill+trea- surer&qid=1679951474&sprefix=bill+treasurer,aps,95&sr=8-4

[12] https://www.amazon.com/Power-Regret-Looking-Backward-Forward/ dp/0735210659/ref=sr_1_1?crid=91V2YVO14BZO&keywords=pow- er+of+regret&qid=1679253368&sprefix=power+of+regret,aps,114&sr=8-1

[13] https://www.amazon.com/Leading-Dignity-Create-Culture-Brings/ dp/0300248458/ref=sr_1_1?crid=1AVKL481DWV0U&keywords=lead- ing+with+dignity+by+donna+hicks+book&qid=1679253405&sprefix=don- na+hicks+le,aps,88&sr=8-1

QUOTES
from the Bravery Survey

"I worked for a tyrant leader for over two years and rather than do anything about it, her behavior caused me to leave and find a new job."

• • •

"I avoided being brave as I didn't fire an employee whose performance was holding us back."

• • •

"I was bullied by a more senior leader, and I was told that raising the issue would cause my career to suffer more than his."

• • •

"I watched a co-worker get bullied and did not do anything about it."

• • •

"I terminated an employee who was demonstrating bad behavior and although I worked with him to help him improve, he's still on my mind as I wonder if more patience and effort to keep him could have been demonstrated."

• • •

"I took a client's perspective on how to solve a problem and did not listen to my gut. The client wasn't right, yet I did not attempt to push back the first time it came up."

CHAPTER FOUR

The Bravery Trick Model©

"People need to be brave enough and courageous enough to articulate a vision."

– **Richard Boyatzis**, *Organizational Theorist,*
University Professor, Author, and Be Brave at Work©
Podcast Guest – Episodes 187 & 188

Since December 2019, I have hosted nearly 300 conversations on my twice-weekly podcast, *Be Brave at Work©*. I've had discussions with individuals such as leadership coach Marshall Goldsmith; *Dignity* and *Leading with Dignity* author Donna Hicks; executive coach Peter Bregman; and professor and academic researcher Richard Boyatzis. All of the business leaders, authors, teachers, leadership professionals, and coaches on my program generously shared their knowledge and experience about being brave at work.

When I began hosting *Be Brave at Work©,* I did not plan to write a book about this topic. Yet, after multiple conversations with educated and experienced guests, I noticed definite themes emerging. And I found that these themes echoed those I had experienced as a corporate employee and as a leadership coach working with hundreds of clients who were seeking ways to be more effective in their workplaces.

Through my experience and research, I have determined that the key to being brave at work focuses on four important areas: practice, presence, future-focus, and flexibility, which I call The Bravery Trick Model© (TBT Model©).

This model comes from many sources: hundreds of hours of listening to my podcast guests reflect on how to be braver at work, sixteen years working as a coach with successful business leaders helping them identify ways to have greater influence and impact, and twenty-five years as a corporate employee working to grow and develop into a corporate leader. In the following chapters, we will identify and explain each element of the model—practice, presence, future-focus, and flexibility—as tools to simply and effectively be brave at work.

In her bestselling book, *Feel the Fear...and Do It Anyway: Dynamic Techniques for Turning Fear, Indecision, and Anger into Power, Action, and Love*, author Susan Jeffers, who was dubbed the "Queen of Self-Help" by the *London Times*, writes, "Pushing through fear is less frightening than living with the underlying fear that comes from a feeling of helplessness. The more helpless we feel, the more severe is the undercurrent of dread that comes with knowing there are situations in life over which we have no control. 'What if' fear permeates our lives."[1]

In this book, *The Bravery Trick*, my goal is to provide you with guidelines that will help you push through fear so that you can lead your colleagues and your organization to be more successful.

Caveat About the TBT Model©

Although I strongly believe that the concepts contained in the TBT Model© will be helpful to you, I also recognize that no model works for everyone. For example, not everyone plays golf the same way. Tiger Woods and Annika Sorenstam are both great golfers yet each one hits the ball completely differently. And not everyone scrambles eggs the same way, either. Some people like to add water or milk while others toss in green peppers and other garnishes.

You may not be ready to be brave at work or, if you are ready, you may approach your conversations in different ways. After reading and understanding the concepts presented in *The Bravery Trick,* especially the TBT Model©, I hope you try these strategies on for size and discover which way to be brave at work is best for you.

Prerequisites for the Success of the TBT Model©

If you are planning to be brave at work by saying something hard to say or hard for your colleague to hear, then these three conditions must be present because they are necessary for the success of the TBT Model©: (1) you have the drive and opportunity to be brave, (2) you are motivated to help a colleague (or two!), and (3) you have a positive relationship with that colleague prior to your bravery conversation. Let's take a look at these prerequisites, one at a time.

The Drive and Opportunity for Bravery at Work

To be brave at work you must commit to bravery and have opportunities in your workplace that call for such behavior. To determine your drive and opportunity for bravery, ask yourself the following three questions:

1. Do I want to promote my personal development, advance my career, improve my leadership style, and provide positive role modeling for my co-workers by being braver at work?

2. On a scale of one (low) to six (high), what is my level of *opportunity* for bravery at work? Not everyone has many opportunities to be brave at work, so it is important to assess the opportunities you have. If you have fewer than one opportunity for bravery a month, score yourself a one. If you find yourself with daily bravery opportunities, score yourself a six.

3. On a scale of one (low) to six (high), how likely am I to *take action* on these opportunities for bravery at work? For this question, we are discussing the likelihood that you will be brave when the opportunity presents itself. If you don't plan to act on opportunities for bravery at work, score yourself a one. If you think you will act on every opportunity for bravery, score yourself a six.

If you answered "Yes" to the first question and scored above a three for each of the next two questions, you have the will and the opportunity to be braver at work.

I currently work with a client named Darnell who wants to invest in his professional development. He wants to learn how best to function as a partner in his firm and as a team leader and is interested in identifying specific actions he can take to help his co-workers. "I can and will do better" is his motto. Darnell obviously wants to find occasions to be brave at work so he can parlay those opportunities into becoming the best leader he can be.

On the other hand, Maria, another one of my clients, is not at all curious about becoming braver at work. As the newly appointed CEO of her organization, she firmly believes that the negative issues she experiences are caused by her colleagues and their organization's culture, not by her. "It's not me—it's them" could be her motto. Maria's lack of desire to invest in personal development and build her self-awareness makes it difficult— if not impossible—for her to affect any positive progress for herself or her company. She is certainly not interested in being brave at work.

ACTION

Within your organization, what opportunities for bravery exist?
What is an activity you could do to create more opportunities to
be brave at work with at least one of your co-workers?

As you search for opportunities for bravery within your organization, keep in mind that moments for bravery happen in one of two ways: unexpectedly and purposefully. Unexpected moments requiring bravery occur when you do not expect them and your response to them must be instantaneous. Many things in life happen unexpectedly and cause you to have a physical response in the moment. Emotions rise and your desire to say something may occur uncontrollably. As Julius Caesar said, "No one is so brave that he is not disturbed by something unexpected." Yet, in anticipation of an unexpected situation, and with experience, you can navigate these troubling emotions effectively. Even though you are not able to plan or strategize for spontaneous challenges, you should still treat them as opportunities for bravery.

The other night, I watched a television show in which a young woman was turned down for an internship at a sophisticated clothing store because of her casual appearance, yet she was given a different justification by the owner. Suspecting the truth, the young woman turned to her friend who was already employed at the store, and asked for her support. Her friend had two choices in that instant: (1) to lie to cover for her boss, or (2) to be brave and support her friend. Unfortunately, she did not choose wisely and thus missed that unexpected opportunity to be brave at work.

Purposeful moments of bravery are planned and scheduled. When you find yourself negatively impacted by another person; you think about what, when, and how you will say something, and you make plans to have the conversation. When asked about the importance of planning, Abraham Lincoln famously said, "Give me six hours to cut down a tree and I will spend the first four hours sharpening the axe." With purposeful moments of bravery, as opposed to unexpected moments, you may have weeks to get ready to say something hard to say or hard for the other person to hear.

A client of mine, Amir, knew he needed to have a brave conversation with his boss about some disruptive behavior his boss was demonstrating. Amir was unsure how his boss would respond. Using the TBT Model© of bravery discussed in this book, Amir carefully prepared for the meeting for six weeks and was ready to be brave when the moment arrived.

ACTION

Identify situations within your organization that may require purposeful moments of bravery from you—when you plan for a brave conversation. When might you encounter an unexpected moment requiring bravery when you would have to react more spontaneously?

Regardless of whether your occasion for workplace bravery is anticipated and planned or completely spontaneous, you can identify it as an opportunity to be brave and be prepared for it. The TBT Model© presented in this book is a method you can use to meet this challenge.

The Motivation to Help Your Colleagues

Another prerequisite to being brave at work is to identify your motivation. Are you looking to make your life easier? Are you trying to solve a problem? Or are you trying to help a colleague? In her 2017 blogpost, "Why Motivation is Important to Life," life and leadership coach Natalie Cook states that motivation does all of the following:

- Clarifies a goal
- Sets priorities in life
- Pushes through setbacks
- Teaches perseverance
- Fights against fear
- Builds self-confidence
- Inspires others[2]

Thus, your motivation for being brave at work matters greatly.

I have found that for the TBT Model© to be most effective, your prime motivator for being brave at work should be to help your colleagues. Sure, you can improve your personal development, advance your career, and work on your leadership style, too—all of the things we mentioned in Chapter 3 as benefits to being brave at work—but the best motivation is to help others do and be better. Being brave at work is not about belittling another person. And it's not about being right. It's about helping colleagues process and understand more than they do today in ways that allows them to influence and impact your organization in positive ways.

ACTION

Think about a difficult workplace conversation you know you need to have but are avoiding. Identify your motivation for saying something hard to say or hard for your colleague to hear that will increase your likelihood for saying something.

A Positive Relationship with Your Colleague

Many business experts discuss the importance of work relationships. In the "Mind Tools Content Team" blog post, "Building Good Work Relationships," the writers state, "The more comfortable co-workers are around one other, the more confident they'll feel voicing opinions, brainstorming, and going along with new ideas. This level of teamwork is essential to embrace change, create, and innovate. And when people see the successes of working together in this way, group morale and productivity soar."[3] Positive relationships are especially vital when it comes to bravely sharing ways of improving with a co-worker. If you have a great relationship with him, he is more likely to listen to you and agree with what you have to say. Conversely, if you don't have a good relationship with him, your effort to be brave will be exponentially harder. If your colleague doesn't know you well, he may think, "Who are you and why should I listen to what you have to say?" Or he may fear that you are criticizing or belittling him. To be brave with a colleague at work, you must first establish a positive relationship with him before sharing your observations and feedback.

I understand that it is not always possible to have a positive relationship with every one of your colleagues. If you do not have a positive relationship with someone yet are motivated to provide her with helpful feedback, you will need to invest some time and energy to improve the relationship first, before bravely trying to help her.

ACTION

Think about a difficult workplace conversation you know you need to have but are avoiding. Do you have a positive relationship with that colleague? If yes, what makes it a positive relationship? If no, what can you do to build a more positive relationship with her before you say something hard to say or hard for her to hear?

Fahrizal was one of two partners in a property management firm. He and Howard went into business together even though they had very different personality styles that often caused them to argue about the simplest of decisions. Fahrizal felt that these recurring arguments were not helping move the company forward, so he often avoided being candid with Howard to avoid disagreements. Over time, Fahrizal found that this lack of candor was creating misunderstandings between him and Howard. He began to be more transparent by openly discussing his reasons for his decisions and encouraging Howard to do the same. As their candor grew, their relationship improved, too, and they were able to discuss issues in a much more positive and constructive way. Today, Fahrizal and Howard continue to be respectfully candid with one another, and their organization is prospering.

As you can see in Fahrizal's example, having a positive relationship with a colleague is a valuable investment of your time and energy since it greatly increases your chances of influencing him in positive ways.

Once you ensure that you have the drive and opportunity to be brave, you are motivated to help a colleague (or two), and you have a positive relationship with that colleague prior to your bravery conversation, you are ready to employ the TBT Model©. Remember, your bravery goals are to prepare for a conversation with a colleague that you believe will be helpful to your colleague's performance and/or reputation (practice); to share what you and others are experiencing based on being fully present (presence); to create the belief with your colleague that she needs to do some things differently to be more effective (future-focus); and to brainstorm and discuss ideas about how to do things differently that will be more effective (flexibility). Where do you start? With the first step of the TBT Model©: practice.

CHAPTER NOTES

[1] https://www.amazon.com/Feel-Fear-Anyway-Techniques-In-decision/dp/0063291290/ref=sr_1_1?crid=XO1FHVKU-HA9V&keywords=feel+the+fear+and+do+it+anyway+susan+jef-fers&qid=1679253990&sprefix=feel+the+f,aps,95&sr=8-1
[2] https://www.nataliecook.com/blog/why-motivation-is-important-in-life
[3] https://www.mindtools.com/aorqe4z/building-good-work-relationships

QUOTES
from the Bravery Survey

"I allowed a toxic leader to rock my belief system which ultimately led to me leaving the organization."

* * *

"I was pressured by a senior executive to break a confidence I had with another employee, which I did. I ended up feeling bad for not having the bravery to say 'No.'"

* * *

"I didn't speak up about a colleague who wasn't qualified to take on a project and the project ended in disaster."

* * *

"My CEO is woefully ineffective in his role, which the board is unable to see, yet I have not said anything proactively to the board."

* * *

"I worked in a high-stakes, high-stress environment, and one day my manager came into my office, threw a stack of papers on the floor, and shouted a series or expletives about the quality of the work. I never broached this topic with him, and I wish I had as I worry that he treats other people this way."

* * *

"A former boss of mine was very aggressive—could be classified as bullying—to my direct reports and although I witnessed the behavior, I did not do anything about it. At least one employee left the company, and our work environment was bad."

CHAPTER FIVE

Practice

"With practice comes reduced discomfort."

–**Sterling Hawkins**, *Author, Keynote Speaker, and* Be Brave at Work© *Podcast Guest – Episode 226*

Practice Makes Perfect

Dylan was an accomplished singer, drummer, bass player, and runner. Yet these achievements did not come easily to him. While he found himself interested in these areas, he needed the discipline to succeed in his efforts. Dylan spent years training his voice, whether alone in his bedroom, for audiences in high school, or as a member of a state-wide band. He fine-tuned his drum- and bass-playing capabilities by spending hours reading music, playing in a high school band, and then transitioning these skills to an ensemble that plays at local bars and weddings. And he practiced running. Lots and lots of running.

Whether at the local track, on the streets of his hometown, or at the top of a 4,000-foot mountain in New Hampshire, Dylan practiced and practiced and practiced. "I could never have achieved any of these accomplishments without hours and hours of practice," Dylan told me. "And this was focused practice; I knew what I wanted to achieve, and I focused on making meaningful progress."

Let's use this definition:

> **Practice:**
> Recurring activities designed to help you
> get better at a skill or behavior

The best way to improve at anything is to practice. In my bravery survey, eighty-three percent of respondents believe they would have been more likely to be brave at work if they had practiced what they wanted to say or do and seventy-nine percent believe that more experience would have increased their likelihood of saying or doing something that required bravery. The more you do it, the better you will become—at anything.

A landmark 1993 study suggested that practice alone accounted for about eighty percent of the difference between an elite performance and an amateur performance.[1] Musicians, athletes, and actors all practice to improve their skills. And if you are making your bed, mowing your lawn, or getting dressed, you too are practicing—knowing how to fold sheets in easier ways, realizing how to access hard places with your lawnmower, and understanding which color shirts and slacks match each other. Each time you do something—every time you practice—you are getting better and better.

But practice requires time and energy. In his book, *Outliers*, author, journalist, and public speaker Malcolm Gladwell states that it takes 10,000 hours of practice to become an expert at something.[2] Based on that, if you wanted to become an accomplished bass player and practiced ten hours each week, becoming an expert would take you almost twenty years. That's a lot of time and energy! At the other end of the spectrum, Josh Kaufman, the author of *The Personal MBA: Master the Art of Business,* suggests expertise can come after just twenty hours of practice.[3] While the amount of time to practice to become skilled at something may vary, the *need* to practice is the common denominator.

And yet practice is not easy. In her 2016 article, "The Importance of Practice – And Our Reluctance to Do It," researcher and author Jennifer Long writes, "Be honest about the difficulty of learning something new, especially when you're in a leadership role. Expect mistakes. Celebrate effort and risk-taking rather than expertise and skill level."[4] In other words, enjoy the practicing as much as—or more than—your end results.

Practice is also imperative to cultivate bravery at work, especially when preparing to have a difficult discussion with someone. This means you'll have to live through the challenging conversation multiple times in advance of actually delivering it. Yuck. It's bad enough to experience a tough conversation once, let alone over and over in practice. Famed Hollywood director Michael Cimino (*The Deer Hunter* and *Heaven's Gate*) was known to have his actors do twenty to thirty takes of a single scene since he believed that practice led to perfection. Whether you believe that to be true or not, practicing for a difficult conversation will prepare you for a much better experience when you take it live.

Three Necessary Steps of Bravery Practice

As you practice bravely saying something that may be hard for you to say or difficult for a colleague to hear, follow these three steps: (1) create talking points versus writing a script, (2) practice with another person, and (3) be open to opportunities for improvement. Let's break down each one of these steps individually.

Create Talking Points Versus Writing a Script

A script is a compilation of words that one or more people say in a specific way and in a specific order. With a script, the conversation goes incredibly smoothly because everyone knows what everyone else is going to say. Unfortunately, this smooth exchange of ideas is impossible in most conversations when not everyone has the same script. For instance, in a bravery conversation, you have no idea how a boss or colleague will react. Will he handle your feedback gracefully? Will he get angry? You cannot completely write out your portion of the conversation when the other person is script-less.

A better tool to use in a bravery conversation is *talking points.* Talking points are a series of thoughts and observations that you want to remember to use in a conversation with another person, regardless of the order in which you say them. You probably wrote them down and practiced them in a specific order ahead of time, yet since your conversation is essentially unpredictable, you might have to jump around your list of talking points a little while you are having your bravery conversation.

If you read my book, *Drive Your Career,* you may recall a story I told about Warren Beatty and Faye Dunaway's misdelivery of the Best Picture winner announcement at the 2017 Oscars. (Yes, you can still see their mistake on YouTube.[5]) If the Academy had provided the two presenters with talking points on how to handle an error such as being given the wrong envelope, the events would have unfolded more positively and professionally.

How to Create Talking Points

To put together talking points, practice the following three steps: (1) get your thoughts out of your head and onto paper, (2) utilize the four-section method, and (3) convert your thoughts to talking points.

Talking Points Step 1:
Get Your Thoughts Out of Your Head and Onto Paper

Face it. A lot is going on in your head. Memories. Observations. Activities. Researchers say that the average adult human brain can store the equivalent of 2.5 million gigabytes of memory.[6] So, when faced with a moment when you need to be brave with another person, your thoughts are at risk of getting lost in the other data, and emotions, floating around in your head. To avoid this, start by finding a little quiet time, think about the upcoming bravery situation, and get your thoughts, observations, and feelings out of your head and onto paper. Don't worry about the order you jot them down in. The goal is to identify the pertinent data you have in your head and document it in one place. Take a few days to do this activity to ensure you remember all of your thoughts and ideas. Some of your perceptions may be evasive, so you are more likely to be able to write down all of them in multiple brain-storming sessions.

Talking Points Step 2: *Utilize the Four-Section Method*

Now that you have written down all of your thoughts, observations, and feelings regarding the topic you wish to discuss with your colleague, your next step is to organize and simplify these random observations into the four elements of your upcoming discussion: the opening, the impact, the motivation, and the next steps.

1. **The Opening**

   Your opening reflects how you want to start your conversation. You want to ensure the person with whom you are speaking knows you are attempting to help her, not to judge or belittle her. Your opening needs to be positive and brief and should avoid extensive set-ups and explanations so that the person you are speaking with doesn't become anxious. After your opening, if your colleague says she is ready to listen and discuss the issue, you can move forward. If your colleague says she isn't ready or interested, you should share with her that your conversation will clarify what you are asking her to hear and you feel it is important for her to hear your observation. If your colleague still says "No," you need to move on and save your energy and effort for a different battle. My experience has shown, however, that a large percentage of colleagues will say "Yes," even if it's just to hear what the concern might be.

2. **The Impact**

   Quickly shift the conversation from the opening to describe the impact your colleague's behavior is having on others. One to three examples are sufficient to help your colleague understand why you have chosen to speak with her. Your examples should be very clear and specific. And remember to ask her why she is behaving the way she is. She might have a legitimate reason for her disruptive behavior.

3. The Motivation

Once you have identified the impact her actions are having on others, shift the discussion to suggestions of some possible solutions to help motivate her to better manage her situation. This is also the time to ask your colleague for her ideas for possible solutions. Understand that she may need a little time to think of some ideas. You could always take a break at this point and schedule part two of the conversation for some time later.

4. Next Steps

Regardless of how your conversation unfolds, you always want to finish by recapping the conversation and focusing on next steps moving forward. This helps ensure your conversation ends by being future-focused. Offer to provide your colleague with a list of the next steps you discussed to ensure she has them documented. Conclude the conversation by thanking her for speaking with you, and for her commitment to exploring possible ways to be different in her interactions with others.

Four-Step Method Example:

Here is a simple example of how you can utilize the Four-Step Method to organize your conversation before converting it into talking points:

1. The opening: "Good morning, Dave. I hope you are doing well. I'd like to provide you with some observations from our meeting this morning. Are you open to hearing them right now?"

2. The impact: "I've noticed over the last four to five meetings that you are often five to ten minutes late, which irritates some of our colleagues because it delays the start of the meetings, and we

frequently can't get to all our agenda items. Can you share with me why you are running late to our meetings so often?"

3. **The motivation:** "I have some suggestions of how you could be more on time in the future. And I'd love to hear your ideas, too."

4. **Next steps:** "Can you share with me the steps you are going to take to be on time going forward? Thank you for listening and your commitment to progress, Dave."

Talking Points Step 3: *Convert Your Thoughts to Talking Points*

Remember that talking points are not a script that tells you exactly what you need to say and the order in which you should say it. Rather, talking points are comments—bullet points—that capture the essence of what you want to say, regardless of the order you use them. They are your reminders to ensure that you say everything you planned to say by the time the conversation is complete.

For example, here is a scripted comment: "Dave, I want to chat with you today about the fact that you are recurringly late for meetings and the negative impact this behavior is having on team productivity and morale." As a talking point, here is how you could write it in your notes to remind you what you want to say: "Dave is late for meetings, and it is having a negative impact."

By using talking points instead of a script, you also are free to change the style and tone of your words so that you connect well and naturally with your colleague.

Talking Points Example

Let's look at an example of talking points for a conversation to have with Dave, your direct report, who is frequently five to ten minutes late for a weekly team meeting.

- Say good morning and ask about his weekend
- Explain why you are there
- Ask Dave if he is okay with hearing this feedback

- Discuss what you have observed that causes you to speak with him today
- Talk about whether this behavior is one-off or recurring
- Ask Dave for his observations of his timeliness
- Thank him for his thoughts
- Find out if he is open to chatting about some ways to ensure he is always on time for your weekly meetings
- Work together to identify one to three possible solutions
- Thank Dave for his thoughts
- Commit to helping him succeed
- Thank Dave again for his openness to chatting about this topic

I recognize that not all conversations may go as smoothly as you would like them to go. Sometimes people will get emotional. Some colleagues will not be open to new ideas or your observations. Some will just defer to defensiveness and the conversation will feel like it is going nowhere. We will chat about handling emotional responses and deviations in Chapter Eight: flexibility.

Practice With Another Person

Practicing your talking points before your bravery discussion is like a pianist working toward his big debut. By the time he performs in front of an audience, he's put in hours of focused practice, much of it spent working with a piano teacher or performance coach. Similarly, if you are planning to have a brave conversation at work, you need to practice with someone else beforehand.

To do this, you need another person—let's call this person a conversation coach—who will carefully listen to your thoughts and provide you with helpful feedback. This coach may be a co-worker who has also experienced the situation you are sharing first-hand. Or perhaps she is a friend who is comfortable listening to your explanation of the problem, hearing your proposed talking points, and then providing you with critical feedback. Most importantly, your coach needs to be someone who will give you honest and constructive feedback.

When presenting your talking points to your conversation coach, ask her to provide feedback based on these questions:

- How do my talking points make you feel?
- Am I being clear in what I am saying?
- Will my talking points help improve the situation?

Continue to work with your coach until you feel ready to move forward.

Be Open to Opportunities for Improvement

As you practice your brave conversation, be open to the feedback you receive from your conversation coach and view it as an opportunity for you to improve your talking points. Perhaps there is a more positive way to start the conversation. Maybe you need to show more curiosity about your colleague's reasons for behaving the way she is behaving. Perhaps you could behave more patiently as you chat with your colleague without trying to rush to an outcome. Practice provides you with the opportunity to work out the kinks in your delivery, which will greatly improve your likelihood of having an effective conversation. As you receive feedback, continue to modify your talking points and continue practicing them with your conversation coach until you feel confident in your delivery.

ACTION

Think about your colleagues at work. Who among them would you ask to be your conversation coach to help you prepare for a brave-at-work conversation?

As we've discussed in this chapter, the first step in the TBT Model© is practice, which deals with creating talking points for your brave discussion, practicing them with another person, and being open to opportunities for improvement suggested to you by your coach. If you follow these steps, like the concert pianist I mentioned earlier, you will have your material well-polished and feel ready to present it to your intended audience.

Now that you have practiced what it is you want to say to be brave at work, it is time to examine the next step of the TBT Model©: presence.

CHAPTER NOTES

[1] https://psycnet.apa.org/buy/1993-40718-001

[2] https://www.amazon.com/Outliers-Story-Success-Malcolm-Gladwell/dp/0316017930/ref=sr_1_1?crid=PWZUR51VTWXY&keywords=outliers&qid=1679254834&sprefix=outliers,aps,95&sr=8-1

[3] https://ideas.ted.com/dont-have-10000-hours-to-learn-something-new-thats-fine-all-you-need-is-20-hours/

[4] https://www.harvardbusiness.org/the-importance-of-practice-and-our-reluctance-to-do-it/

[5] https://www.youtube.com/watch?v=s86NgOVGlo0

[6] https://www.medanta.org/patient-education-blog/what-is-the-memory-capacity-of-a-human-brain/

QUOTES
from the Bravery Survey

"I should have pushed back against groupthink and I did not."

. . .

"I've not said something aloud because I feared sounding inexperienced and stupid."

. . .

"I challenged someone who was better prepared on the subject, and I should have practiced and been even better prepared."

. . .

"I was not brave by not pushing a project to be a higher priority, which resulted in delays in our ability to effectively capitalize on the idea."

. . .

"By not being brave, I created significant stress on myself."

. . .

"I was working as a temp for a non-profit organization that was misleading the public in its reporting of the percentage of donations that went back to the public. I did not say anything as I feared I would lose my job."

CHAPTER SIX

Presence

"We tend to think, 'How is this going to reflect on me?' or 'How am I going to be perceived?' and these are not the right places to have your thoughts. It is about the person with whom you are speaking and/or representing."

– **Harry Ebbighausen**, *Former President Iron Mountain Records Management and* Be Brave at Work©
Podcast Guest – Episodes 1 & 2

What is Presence?

Let me tell you the stories of three clients who were trying to improve their experiences in their organizations. Each of them was seeking ways to be seen accurately in their company yet the nature of their searches varied.

Angie was the senior vice president of marketing for a consumer financial services firm. She had been in her role for about a year and, based on feedback from others, she believed that she needed greater presence when she entered a room or connected with others. When I asked her what leadership presence looked like to her, she had a hard time answering my question.

As a manufacturing executive in an automobile accessory firm, Katya led multiple teams in her organization. Katya told me she wanted to work on her presence so it would be clearer to others that she was the key decision-maker. When I asked Katya what executive presence looked like to her, she also struggled to find a response.

Carlo was a pharmaceutical engineer in a large biotech company working on a treatment for colon cancer. He had big aspirations for his career and told me he wanted to demonstrate greater presence when working with others. When I asked him what greater presence looked like to him, his response was vague and unclear.

Why is defining presence so difficult? In her book, *Presence,* professor and social psychologist Amy Cuddy writes, "We know it when we feel it, and we know it when we see it, but presence is hard to define." And this is at the beginning of her book! Ms. Cuddy then offers her definition of presence, which speaks directly to demonstrating bravery at work: "[Presence is] the state of being attuned to and able to comfortably express our true thoughts, feelings, values, and potential." She goes on to say, "Presence stems from believing our own stories. When we don't believe our stories, we are inauthentic—we are deceiving, in a way, both ourselves and others. And this self-deception is, it turns out, observable to others as our confidence wanes and our verbal and nonverbal behaviors become dissonant."[1] Presence is necessary to be a good co-worker and a good leader.

> **Presence:**
> Your ability to be seen, heard, felt, and recognized as the expert in your area of interest.

Using this as our definition, let's look at presence as it pertains to being brave at work.

Being Attuned to Others

Harry Ebbighausen was the president of a division of Iron Mountain, the world's largest records management company and my first *Be Brave at Work*© podcast guest (Episodes 1 & 2). Harry was known for treating everyone with dignity and respect, and for providing constructive feedback. When meeting with a colleague, he sat next to the person at a side table, not behind his desk. He put his office phone on mute and left his cellphone and laptop on his desk. He had a sheet of paper and a pen available to take notes. He demonstrated curiosity. He listened. And he problem-solved *with* the person, not *for* her. This was a leader who demonstrated great presence and was fully attuned to the needs of others. Co-workers felt as though Harry was on a journey with them.

Harry's behavior is rare in the business world. More often, when a boss speaks to employees, he seems rushed, his office phone rings disruptively, he takes recurring peeks at his cellphone, and perhaps he even sends messages during the meeting. If someone knocks on the door, he interrupts the conversation to start another one. The employee doesn't feel as though her boss is on a journey with her because of his lack of presence.

Two Types of Presence

For a conversation to be effective, both parties must be consciously present in two ways: operationally and strategically. Let's discuss both types.

Operational Presence

When you are being brave at work, there are operational aspects of the interaction that must exist to ensure both parties in the conversation are fully focused. Operational presence concerns the more tangible aspects of an effective conversation—ways of doing versus behaving. Here are some components of operational presence:

- **Location:** When thinking about the importance of location, consider this old joke:

  911 Operator: "How can I help you?"

  Voice on the phone: "I need an ambulance. I was just struck by a car."

  911 Operator: "What street are you on sir?"

  Voice on the phone: "I am on Eucalyptus Raisin Street."

  911 Operator: "Can you spell that for me, sir?"

  There is an extended pause.

  911 Operator: "Sir?"

  Voice on the phone: "I'll call you right back. I'm going to drag myself over to Pine Street."

  When you are being brave at work, *where* you meet will affect your outcome significantly. Meeting in your office or your boss's office may feel uncomfortable for the visitor. Cornering someone while she is standing in line waiting to purchase her lunch will never work. Instead, you want to find an effective and objective location so both you and your colleague can be focused and present in the conversation. Typically, the best location is a meeting or conference room, which is free of distractions and provides plenty of space, light, and air.

- **Seating:** When people are having a discussion in a business setting, they often sit across the table from one another in what is referred to as the "competitive/defensive" position. As described on the **www.westsidecoastmasters.com** website, "...in this arrangement, competitors (and colleagues) face each other, just like Western gunslingers. Sitting across the table from a person can create a defensive, competitive atmosphere, and can lead to each party taking a firm stand on his/her point of view because the table becomes a solid barrier between each party."[2] When having a bravery conversation with a coworker, you are not there to compete or defend; you are there to help. To accomplish this, it is better to sit next to your colleague, in what experts call the "cooperative" position. This will increase the likelihood that your colleague will work with you and support your efforts.

When having a conversation with one of his co-workers, Harry, the Iron Mountain executive I mentioned at the start of this chapter, always moved from his chair behind his desk and came over and sat at a table situated at the front of his office, next to her. This ensured Harry neutralized the impression of power, was at eye level with his colleague, and thus connected more effectively.

- **Time of Day:** As Benjamin Franklin famously said, "Early to bed and early to rise makes a person healthy, wealthy, and wise." While this has been proven to be statistically untrue, it reminds us that some colleagues are more attentive in the morning, and some are better in the afternoon. Determining your colleague's best time of day is important to ensure she is present to hear your feedback. If you or your colleague is tired, distracted, or has a low energy level, your bravery discussion won't have the impact you want.

  If you are unsure of what time of day is best for a colleague, ask her: "Hey, Jama. Are you a morning person or an afternoon person? I have some information I want to share with you, and I want to do it at a time that is best for you." By selecting the best time of day for your discussion with your colleague, you will ensure that your comments are heard by her as effectively as possible.

- **Distraction Avoidance:** Today's workplaces are filled with distractions: cellphones, *office phones,* laptops, desktop computers, and other meeting interrupters. Sometimes our colleague's office space can feel like Grand Central Station, which is why it might not be the best place to hold a bravery meeting. By utilizing a meeting or conference room instead, you can significantly reduce many of these common distractions, which is vital to ensure you and your colleague are fully present for your conversation.

Strategic Presence

When Harry, the Iron Mountain executive, met with colleagues, he was purposefully operational *and* intentionally strategic, because he knew that an effective conversation is an elegant blend of tangible and intangible elements. Strategic presence focuses on intangible conversational behaviors needed to have the desired impact you are seeking and refers to ways of *behaving* versus *doing*. Let's look at some strategically present behaviors that are necessary for bravery discussions.

- **Curiosity:** Most great leaders and change agents ask a lot of questions. Inventor Thomas Edison, NASA mathematician Katherine Johnson, and scientist Marie Curie all furthered their works, impact, and influence by being perpetually curious. As Albert Einstein often said, "The important thing is to never stop questioning."

  Donald Latumahina, the founder of Life Optimizer, a self-improvement blog designed to help people reach their full potential, identifies four reasons curiosity is important. First of all, curiosity helps your mind be active versus passive. Your mind is like a muscle that becomes stronger with continual exercise, such as the mental gymnastics caused by curiosity. Secondly, curiosity helps your mind recognize new ideas. When you are curious about something, your mind anticipates and expects to receive new ideas, whereas a person not demonstrating curiosity probably won't notice new or fresh ways to see things. Thirdly, curiosity opens up new possibilities that are hidden below the surface of normal life. It takes curiosity to look more deeply and discover them. Lastly, curiosity brings excitement into your life. Colleagues who are not curious may be susceptible to boring and standard outcomes. Curiosity brings fresh and fun ideas that create excitement and new outcomes.[3]

  To be fully present at a meeting, you must be open and curious about your colleague's thoughts and expectations. Otherwise, you may not be as receptive as you could be, which would decrease the effectiveness of the discussion. Remember author Stephen Covey's recommendation in his milestone book, *The Seven Habits of Highly Effective People*, "Seek first to understand, then to be understood."[4] Stay curious!

- **Listening:** To be curious, you must be an active listener. This doesn't mean being quiet, nodding frequently, and uttering an occasional "uh hum." Active listening is demonstrating to the speaker that you understand her thoughts and perspectives, regardless of whether you agree with her or not. Here are three tips on how to be an active listener:

1. Take notes of the main points in the conversation. This will help you accurately recall comments.

2. Make sure your posture demonstrates active listening. Lean in and be comfortably close to your colleague. This will inspire candor in the conversation.

3. Provide periodic recaps of the items being discussed. You might say, "If I can pause you for a second, Hamish, as I want to be sure I am following you. I hear you saying that..." This ensures you are correctly understanding him.

As Peter Bregman, CEO of Bregman Partners, a multi-book author, and a *Be Brave at Work*© podcast guest (Episodes 98 & 99) states in his book, *Leading with Emotional Courage*, "It turns out that sometimes, just listening is problem-solving. People will want you to trust and be curious about them. When you are, they are received and connected to you. Listening to them is one way to do that."[5] People want to be heard.

• **Note Taking:** When having a bravery conversation with a colleague, take notes of the key points discussed. This is a great way to ensure you capture your colleague's words accurately, as well as to help you remember valuable ideas and comments. Plus, when you want to revisit a point, you can read the comment from your notes versus trying to recall it from memory.

• **Observing:** During your bravery discussion, observe body and facial mannerisms as these can assist you in understanding your colleague's mood or receptivity. By carefully monitoring facial expressions, body movements, and even your coworker's posture, you can ensure he is fully present with you in your conversation. These same clues can also inform you when it is time to take a break or pursue your discussion from a different angle.

For example, if your colleague is leaning toward you, looking you in the eye, and nodding at your comments, then chances are he is present and receptive to your ideas. If, however, he is leaning back in his chair, looking out the window, and shaking his head, then you and your colleague are probably not on the same page.

- **Empathy:** In her book, *Dare to Lead*, bestselling author, speaker, and host of the fifth-most watched TedTalk in history (over 61 million views)[6], Brené Brown writes, "Empathy is not connecting to an experience. Empathy is connecting to the emotions that underpin an experience."[7] To be fully present in any conversation, you must demonstrate that you understand the other person's feelings on the topic, regardless of whether or not you agree with him. If you only focus on the topic and disregard how the other person feels, your conversation will be unfruitful.

In a recent survey completed by Catalyst, a non-profit organization focused on building workplaces that work for women, empathy was shown to positively impact the workplace in the following ways:

- **Innovation:** Sixty-one percent of respondents who said they had empathetic leaders felt able to be innovative at work, compared to thirteen percent who reported to less empathetic leaders.

- **Engagement:** Seventy-six percent of people who experienced empathy from their leaders reported they were engaged and cared about their jobs, compared to only forty-three percent who experienced less empathy from their boss.

- **Inclusivity:** Fifty percent of people with empathetic leaders felt their workplace was inclusive, compared to only seventeen percent of those with less empathetic leadership.[8]

These statistics show you can help a colleague feel more engaged and innovative, and that she is a member of the team by being empathetic during conversations with her. No telling. No judging. No being right. Just understanding how the other person feels, regardless of whether or not you agree with her.

Cultural Awareness and Sensitivity

Most workplaces include individuals from different races, ages, backgrounds, sexual preferences, values, beliefs, and/or presentation styles. A colleague may be from another country, wear unusual clothes, shake hands differently, or be diverse in some other way, and these differences may make you hesitant to say something to him that is hard to say or might be hard to hear. Or perhaps one of these cultural differences is the topic you need to discuss with him. You are afraid of being deemed culturally insensitive or rude. So, rather than taking the chance of offending your colleague, you avoid an important conversation.

The vast majority of us are not experts in cultural awareness and sensitivity. Like bravery, these are not topics traditionally taught in school. Despite this, however, your colleagues expect you to act with cultural awareness and sensitivity. Here are some points to consider in preparation for a conversation where cultural differences may be evident:

- **Ensure you are aware of any cultural differences that might exist.** This may sound obvious, yet you may be so focused on what you need to say to your colleague, you might not think enough about his choices and characteristics.

- **Investigate your colleague's status to build your knowledge base.** Google the topic or speak with another colleague to ensure you operate from a place of knowledge, not ignorance. Afterall, the characteristic or behavior your colleague demonstrates may be for a cultural reason. Obtaining this information beforehand will be helpful to ensure your conversation is meaningful and thoughtful.

- **Do not bring up the cultural difference in your meeting if you don't have to.** If your cultural difference is not relevant to the conversation you are having with your colleague, don't mention it. However, if your colleague brings up the cultural difference or if the reason for your conversation is an acknowledged cultural difference, demonstrate curiosity and listen carefully to ensure you understand her situation fully. This is a great opportunity to practice empathy to ensure your colleague knows she is being seen and heard for who she is and who wants to be.

Commisceo Global's website article, "What Are Some Examples of Cultural Awareness?"[9], provides an example of a positive cultural awareness outcome. An American leader was working with some Japanese colleagues in Japan, and although she did not experience any particular difficulty working with them, she always felt like an outsider. She suspected that cultural differences could be at play, so she did some research. When she learned that in Japan, socializing, going out for drinks, and singing karaoke are ways to build trust, she began joining her colleagues for post-work activities, had a drink with them now and again, and even sang karaoke—although she self-admittedly was horrible. Very soon, she experienced a change in how she was treated and began to feel included. By becoming more aware of her colleagues' cultural differences, she was able to adapt her behavior and fit in better.

Do not avoid having a challenging conversation with a colleague due to the existence of a cultural difference. Instead, focus on the behavior on which you want to provide feedback, be curious, listen, and show empathy. By demonstrating such cultural awareness and sensitivity, your likelihood of success will only grow.

Motivate Your Colleague to Discuss the Topic You Want to Share

Before you say something to a colleague that is hard to say or will be hard for your colleague to hear, you must first motivate him to discuss the topic with you. Otherwise, he might think, "Why would I want to hear solutions to something that I don't see or understand?" If he is thinking that, your likelihood of making positive progress with your brave conversation is low.

You can motivate your colleague to talk about a topic with this simple statement and two questions: "I would like to share an experience that some of us in the office are having with you. Would you be open to hearing more about this topic? And then, if you become curious about what I am sharing, would you be willing to discuss some ideas about possible ways to do something differently?" If your colleague says "Yes," he is motivated and ready to move forward with your discussion. If he says "No," let him know that your conversation with him will clarify what you are talking about. If your colleague still says "No," then drop the subject, at least for the time being. Without his buy-in to the conversation, your conversation will probably not be productive.

In a challenging conversation with a colleague, you must ensure you both are "all in" and present. Beforehand, select the best location, time of day, and seating arrangement, and minimize potential distractions. During the conversation, be curious, listen well, take notes, observe your colleague's reaction to your comments, and show empathy. By being present in these ways, your brave workplace discussion will have optimal chances of success.

Now that we have discussed ways to practice what you want to say and the importance of demonstrating presence with your colleague, it is time to talk about the next step of the TBT Model©: future-focus.

CHAPTER NOTES

[1] www.amazon.com/Presence-Bringing-Boldest-Biggest-Challenges/dp/0316256587/ref=sr_1_1?crid=Q2RLAZKWU7I1&keywords=amy+cuddy&qid=1679247526&sprefix=amy+cuddy,aps,98&sr=8-1

[2] westsidetoastmasters.com/resources/book_of_body_language/chap17.html

[3] www.lifeoptimizer.org/2010/03/31/the-power-of-curiosity/

[4] www.amazon.com/Habits-Highly-Effective-People-Powerful/dp/1982137274/ref=sr_1_1?crid=16VRJXLCDXRET&keywords=seven+habits+of+highly+effective+people+by+stephen+covey&qid=1679253097&sprefix=seven+habi,aps,93&sr=8-1

[5] www.amazon.com/Leading-Emotional-Courage-Conversations-Accountability/dp/1119505690/ref=sr_1_1?crid=T3YUSFD2VWB4&keywords=peter+bregman+leading&qid=1679256333&sprefix=peter+bregman+leading,aps,109&sr=8-1

[6] www.ted.com/talks/brene_brown_the_power_of_vulnerability

[7] www.amazon.com/Dare-Lead-Brave-Conversations-Hearts/dp/0399592520/ref=sr_1_1?crid=2T8OZ8YJ1KBAT&keywords=dare+to+lead+brene+brown&qid=1679952111&sprefix=dare+to+lea,aps,88&sr=8-1

[8] www.catalyst.org/reports/empathy-work-strategy-crisis/

[9] www.commisceo-global.com/blog/what-are-some-examples-of-cultural-awareness

QUOTES
from the Bravery Survey

"The president of a company I worked for would ask for our opinions and often reacted quite intensely to the opinions offered to him. Rather than be brave and help him, I learned not to speak up at meetings."

. . .

"By not being brave, I believe I prolonged my unpleasant employment with my organization."

. . .

"A client made a disparaging remark about a minority group and while I am not a member of this group and neither was anyone present, I did not say anything. Upon reflection, I think I should have."

. . .

"I did not speak up at a meeting where leaders were making hiring decisions based on the race of the candidates. I avoided an uncomfortable conversation which did not help me to make an impact at the organization."

. . .

"I have passed up many opportunities to market myself more aggressively as I fear rejection."

. . .

"I asked a co-worker to align with our organizational documented workflows and she got angry and yelled at me. Rather than do anything or say anything about it, I let it pass and moved on."

CHAPTER SEVEN

Future-Focus

"If you tie collaboration and empathy back to the business, it must be a good thing – look what it does!"

  – **Carol Vallone Mitchell**, *Researcher, Leadership Advisor,*
Co-Founder of Talent Strategy Partners and Be Brave at
Work© *Podcast Guest –Episodes 51, 52, 106, & 107*

Wrongly Focusing on the Past

Lucy worked as the chief financial officer at an information management company where she was becoming increasingly frustrated with the CEO's behavior during meetings. Regardless of the topic or the person speaking, Bill repeatedly interrupted the speaker and interjected off-topic ideas, observations, and recommendations that severely disrupted the meeting's agenda. Lucy believed Bill's behavior was counterproductive and felt she should provide him with some feedback.

The subsequent conversation Lucy initiated did not go well. When she shared examples with Bill of how he was disrupting meetings, he defended himself with long-winded explanations of his past behavior. Lucy and Bill allowed the meeting to become a discussion of good and bad behavior and were so stuck reliving the past, that they did not come up with any ideas or steps he could take to improve his future meeting behavior. Thus, rather than their conversation helping Bill evolve into a more effective leader, as she intended, Lucy felt the conversation was not helpful and damaged their ongoing working relationship.

Focusing on the past is a natural human behavior, even though it is often not a productive way to improve your work environment. To understand why it is important to think about the future as a strategy to help versus the past, we first need to understand why we enjoy remembering the past so much and examine some of the problems regarding our memories.

Why We Enjoy Memories

In an article for *Psychology Today*, psychiatrist Dr. Chris Heath writes, "Memories make us who we are. They create our worldview in ways we hardly realize. Like a character made of Legos, we're built of blocks of memory that all fit together to form our consciousness. How can it be otherwise? How can we say hello to someone or lean in to kiss someone new without evoking memories of previous greetings and kisses? The way it feels to you—your hopes, expectations, and fears—are all built upon what you've experienced before."[1] Your memories document the experience you have had that made you who you are today. These memories also provide you with the information you need to navigate your future.

And we love our memories because they allow us to relive the good times. In the website article, "The Power of Positive Memories: Why Looking Back Makes Us Happier Now," picture frame vendor Aura quotes the work of licensed psychologist Dr. Krystine Batchco, who studies the psychology of nostalgia: "Revisiting the past brings back the joy of the good times and the comforting security of being reunited with loved ones. Happy memories remind us of when life was less complicated. During difficult periods like the one we experienced in 2020, positive recollections strengthen our confidence that life will be good again one day and that we will be able to overcome current challenges and any that come our way."[2] Don't you love reflecting on the "Good ole days," or "When I grew up..." or "Back in the day..."?

Problems With Memories

Yet, there are problems in the ways we remember. In his book, *The Seven Sins of Memory: How the Mind Forgets and Remembers*, author and former Chair of Harvard University's Psychology Department Dr. Daniel Schacter shares that, "Despite memory's obvious benefits, it can also let us down. Memory, for all that it does for us every day and for all of the feats that can sometimes amaze us, can also be a troublemaker."[3] Memories can be faulty or deceptive, which may cause problems. For example, Dr. Schacter's seven sins of memory include negatively influencing behaviors such as bias, absent-mindedness, and temporary inaccessibility.

Many psychologists believe it is harder to forget a bad memory than a good one because negative emotions like fear and sadness trigger increased activity in a part of the brain linked to memories. These emotionally charged memories are preserved in greater detail than happy or more neutral memories, but they may also be subject to distortion. For example, if a group of employees attends a presentation by the president of their company, after the meeting when folks gather at the watercooler, each of the employees will have a different memory of what the president said.

While we all enjoy an occasional trip down memory lane because of the beneficial effects of memories, we need to remain mindful that those memories may not be a completely accurate representation of what happened. Therefore, when being brave at work by working to solve a problem, it is best not to focus on memories of the past, but to look to the future instead.

The Benefits of Being Future-Focused

When we reflect on the past, we think about what was and what could have been. While some of these memories may be positive and helpful, others may prompt non-productive feelings of regret. As psychotherapist Tim Hill states, "When we think about the past in terms of the regrets we have, we are ruminating. At those times, where we think about the past and we wonder what we might have done differently, or we wonder about the actions of others, we are essentially spinning our wheels."[4] So, concentrating on memories of the past probably won't help us resolve current issues we are having at work. Rather, remaining future-focused allows us to consider new options available to us.

> **Future-Focus:**
> Your ability to focus energy and effort on what might be and encourage your colleague to believe he needs to evolve to be more effective.

In her online blog at the Peeler Associates website, leadership coach Marie Peeler writes about how some discussions about the past are misrepresented as being future-focused. "Sometimes, the propensity to talk about the past is more subtle. The conversation sounds like it is about the present, when in reality it is about the past until now. Statements that start with 'We've always...' or 'We don't have...' are really statements about what we've always done in the past until now or what we've not had in the past until now."[5] It is important to avoid this trap and remain future-focused.

Keeping in mind the importance of being future-focused, let's look at three important areas to consider when you are being brave at work: reflection versus remembrance, past versus future transitions, and the concept of feedforward.

Reflection Versus Remembrance

When you are trying to resolve a conflict with a coworker, you or your colleague may be tempted to dredge up and ruminate on memories of past experiences. However, when you are brave at work, you will be more effective if you *reflect* on the past rather than *remember* it. *Reflection* is defined as "continued consideration, meditation, or contemplation to demonstrate the capacity for judging rationally."[6] Let's look at definitions for those three words.

- **Consideration** is defined as "careful thought, deliberation, and thoughtfulness for other people"[6] and is something that needs to be thought over carefully before deciding or acting.

- **Meditation** is defined as "engaging in contemplation or reflection or engaging in a mental exercise to reach a heightened level of spiritual awareness."[6]

- **Contemplation** is defined as "the action of looking thoughtfully at something for a longer amount of time."[6]

Therefore, *reflection* involves viewing your past experiences objectively using *consideration, meditation,* and *contemplation,* and then using logical analysis to learn from them.

Remembrance is defined as "the act of remembering something,"[6] which means mentally re-experiencing it. As we discussed earlier, memory can be seriously affected by many unintentional behaviors such as blocking, suggestibility, and bias, which can negatively impact your ability to recollect the event accurately. If you need to review past behaviors while having a brave discussion with a colleague, reflection is a more effective strategy than remembrance since reflection allows you to recall the past for purposes of consideration and rational judgment versus simply reliving a remembrance.

My clients often report very different remembrances of interactions with their bosses. For example, after an executive leadership meeting, Denise thought their boss, Kenisha, had exercised her authority effectively while David remembered Kenisha's behavior as being negative and de-energizing. Same event. Two differing memories. However, if

Denise and David reflected on their boss's behavior using consideration, meditation, and contemplation, their perspectives would probably have been much more similar. Together, they may have concluded, "Perhaps our boss was behaving at that moment in a way that she needed to behave, yet will not repeat that behavior in the future. Let's observe how she acts going forward to see if this is true." In this situation—and many workplace scenarios—reflection is a more helpful tool than remembrance.

Future Transitions Versus Past Events

Framing your brave conversation with your colleague with a focus on the future versus the past is critical and often can be accomplished by making sure your focus is on the behavior you want to see (the future) versus discussing behavior that is not working (the past). By focusing on the future, you provide others with helpful direction on how you want them to behave.

For example, one of my clients, Cornell, told me he attended a post-conference debriefing session where the conference leader, John, focused his comments on everything that had not gone according to plan. By the time John was halfway through his list, my client and his colleagues were irritated and de-energized. John's observations would have been better received if instead, he had shared his ideas in the form of possible changes to make for the next conference to ensure a better outcome.

When speaking with colleagues, focusing on the future can often be accomplished by using the correct phrases. Here are some examples of possible ways to transition your words from the past to the future:

Instead of saying: *"You are late to work every day."*
You could say: *"I need you to be on time to work on a daily basis."*

Instead of saying: *"You should not talk to your colleagues that way."*
You could say: *"When you speak with your colleagues, ensure you are always respectful and professional."*

Instead of saying: *"Clients hate it when you do not call them back."*

You could say: *"Please ensure you return any calls from your clients daily. If the client does not answer, please leave a message."*

Instead of saying: *"You are a terrible meeting leader."*

You could say: *"Can I provide you some feedback on your meeting leadership skills that I think you would want to hear?"*

By focusing on future behavior, you are emphasizing what you want your colleague to do, which provides your colleague with positive ideas, rather than focusing on his past mistakes, which he can't do anything about.

Feedforward Versus Feedback

Leadership coach, professor, and speaker Marshall Goldsmith suggests we offer our colleagues *feedforward* instead of *feedback*. In his article for *Inc. Magazine*, titled "Instead of Feedback, Try Feedforward to Boost Team Performance," Marshall writes that while feedback provides information about how someone is presently performing, feedforward replaces those positive or negative observations with future-oriented solutions, which are much more helpful and valuable. Mr. Goldsmith then includes a list of several benefits of feedforward.[7] Let's take a close look at some of these benefits.

- **It can change the future:** Feedforward helps your colleagues envision and focus on a positive future, not a failed past. By giving your colleagues ideas on how they can be even more successful, you increase their chances of achieving this success in the future.

- **It is more productive to help your colleagues learn to be right than to prove they were wrong:** Feedback often becomes an exercise in proving someone was wrong in what she said or did. Feedforward is almost always viewed as a positive experience because it focuses on solutions, not problems.

- **People do not take feedforward as personally as feedback:** In theory, constructive feedback focuses on performance, not the person. In practice, however, almost all feedback is taken personally, no matter how it is delivered. Feedforward is not perceived as a personal critique since it discusses something that has not yet happened.

- **We hate getting negative feedback and we don't like giving it either:** When I ask my clients to name two or three things their bosses believe they could be doing differently to be more effective, the vast majority of them do not have an answer. Their bosses have never provided them with this information and my clients have never asked for it. This is because most people don't enjoy giving or receiving constructive feedback, to the point that they avoid it altogether.

- **Feedforward tends to be much faster and more efficient than feedback:** An excellent technique for giving feedforward ideas to a successful person is to say, "Here are four ideas for the future. Please accept these in the positive spirit that they are given and ignore what doesn't make sense for you." That person is then free to evaluate the suggestions on her own time and to adopt the ones she feels are most promising. By using this method of providing feedforward information, no time is wasted on debating the quality of the ideas or proving their validity.

- **Your colleagues will listen more attentively to feedforward than feedback:** During feedback, your co-worker is not fully listening to your thoughts since their brain is spending energy composing their response. In feedforward, he can listen fully and his response can be as simple as "Thank you."

ACTION

Think about the advice you would like to share with one of your colleagues. How could you phrase it as feedforward versus feedback?

Michael was tasked with providing Roger with some thoughts on difficulties co-workers were experiencing with him. Michael knew this information would be hard for Roger to hear and was worried that the conversation would not go well. Michael decided to present the information as feedforward, with a focus on how Roger needed to behave for others to experience him better. Michael met with Roger, shared a couple of examples of how his behavior was experienced as being disruptive by others, and then quickly shifted to feedforward ideas on how Roger could behave to have a more positive impact on others. The conversation went well, and Roger committed to improving his behavior at work.

Reflecting on the past is something we are all drawn to do. Yet when you are being brave at work by discussing a challenging topic with a colleague, it is critical to focus your time and energy on the future. This is because all the solutions to our problems exist in the future.

In the previous chapters, we have identified ways to practice what you want to say or do, the importance of being present with your colleague, and the need to focus your conversation on future behaviors. Let's now talk about the final step of the TBT Model©: flexibility.

CHAPTER NOTES

[1] https://www.psychologytoday.com/us/blog/psychoanalysis-un-plugged/201708/your-memories-make-you-who-you-are

[2] https://auraframes.com/blog/the-power-of-positive-memories-why-looking-back-makes-us-happier-now#:~:text=Krystine%20Batcho%2C%20PhD%2C%20who%20studies,when%20life%20was%20less%20complicated.

[3] https://www.apa.org/monitor/oct03/sins

[4] https://www.bustle.com/p/why-do-we-feel-nostalgia-a-new-study-says-it-has-more-to-do-with-sadness-than-you-think-17015765

[5] https://peelerassociates.com/to-make-things-happen-focus-on-the-future-not-the-past/

[6] https://www.wordnik.com/words/

[7] https://www.inc.com/marshall-goldsmith/power-of-feedforward.html

QUOTES
from the Bravery Survey

"Not being brave at work has made me feel inferior."

. . .

"I should have gone to the head of my work unit to tell him that my manager was a bully and behaved in a biased way, yet I did not do so."

. . .

"I avoided reacting to a situation where a patron had too much to drink. Not addressing that in front of my staff set a bad precedent and stays with me until today."

. . .

"A leader consistently behaved poorly, yet I did not hold him to the same standard I used for other employees as he was more senior than me. This hurt the level of trust my employees had in me."

. . .

"My team and I decided not to accept a proposal and yet during the meeting with senior management, I accepted it. I let down my team and to this day, I still regret it."

. . .

"I allowed senior voices to overpower my voice, even though I thought I was right, yet I was afraid of not pleasing them. I was not brave in my interactions, and we ultimately compromised the design in ways that needed to be fixed after implementation."

CHAPTER EIGHT

Flexibility

"I always say that in founding Constant Contact, we were on the East Coast and we worked in the attic. If we were on the West Coast, we would have had a garage!"

– **Alec Stern**, *Entrepreneur, Speaker, Mentor, Investor, Co-Founder of Constant Contact and* Be Brave at Work© *Podcast Guest – Episode 50*

Someone Who Always Has to be Right

Amit's colleagues said he acted as if he believed there were only two ways to view every topic: his way and his way. They experienced him as someone who always shared his opinion, always had to be right, and always fought any view different than his own. Amit's perceived inflexibility created the belief that any suggestions provided to him would fall on deaf ears. Hence, no one ever provided him feedback or feedforward information. Ever. Whenever Amit shared his opinions with others, he would do so very adamantly and, as a colleague put it, he "would never back down." Amit acted as if his perspective of every topic was the *only* correct answer. He was so inflexible that his co-workers discounted him, never asking for his opinion or listening to his advice.

ACTION
Do you have any colleagues who remind you of Amit—who always have to be right? What effect does their behavior have on your team?

You Don't Always Have the Right Answer

When preparing for a conversation with a colleague in which you plan to discuss how he could be more effective, you will often identify what you consider to be the perfect answer, saying to yourself, "I know what he should do!" However, when you actually speak with that colleague, keep in mind that many solutions might help him make progress, not just the one you came up with before your conversation. Remember that you are not your colleague and—based on his unique background and experiences—he may choose to move forward in a different way than the one you envisioned.

Part of your job in helping co-workers improve through brave conversations is realizing that you don't always have the right answer. As Melody Stanford Martin, a social ethicist, founder and CEO of the Cambridge Creative Group, and *Be Brave at Work©* podcast guest (Episodes 111 & 112) writes in her book, *Brave Talk: Building Resilient Relationships in the Face of Conflict,* "When you seek to support someone going through difficulties, the first step is to stop doing anything that draws attention to yourself or your ideas. Stop talking about yourself, don't share your solution at the start of the conversation, and stop referencing yourself. This is about them. Your goal is to get them to talk."[1] The plan going forward that results from the conversation with your co-worker must be something that he—not you—are comfortable implementing.

More Than One Correct Answer

In his bestselling book on the creative mind, *A Whack on the Side of the Head*, Roger von Oech provides an exercise that demonstrates the variability of the correct answer. He presents the following five figures and instructs the reader to select the one that is different from the others:

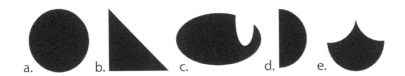

As von Oech states, "If you chose Figure B, congratulations! You've picked the right answer. Figure B is the only one that has all straight lines. Give yourself a pat on the back! Some of you, however, may have chosen Figure C, thinking that C is unique because it's the only one that is asymmetrical (having parts that fail to correspond to one another in shape, size, or arrangement). You are also right! C is the right answer. A case can also be made for Figure A: it's the only one with no points. Therefore, A is the right answer. What about Figure D? It is the only one that has both a straight line and a curved line. So, D is the right answer too. And Figure E? Among other things, E is the only one that looks like a projection of a non-Euclidean triangle (where only one line can go through a given point and can be parallel to a given line) into a Euclidean space. It is also the right answer. In other words, they are all right depending on your point of view."[2] As Mr. Von Oech so clearly demonstrates, there is more than one correct answer to most questions.

In our discussion of the TBT Model©, we will use this definition of flexibility:

Flexibility:
Being open to giving and considering new ideas and solutions to move a situation forward in positive ways

The concept of flexibility includes the notion that there is seldom one correct solution to any given problem, a fact that must be clear to you and your colleague for a productive conversation to occur.

People Like Choices

In a behavioral study led by Daniel Mochon, an associate professor at Tulane University, participants were divided into three groups and asked to purchase DVD players.[3] The first group was presented with a single option: to buy a Sony DVD player. The second group was also given a single option: to buy a Philips DVD player. The third group was presented with the opportunity to choose either a Sony or a Philips DVD player. Just nine percent of the first group and ten percent of the second group showed any intention of buying a DVD player. This meant that at least ninety percent of those groups did not want to buy one. In the third group, however, thirty-two percent chose the Sony DVD player and thirty-four percent chose the Philips DVD player. That is a 650 percent increase in the buyer conversion rate. Why? Because the third group had more than one option. The study showed that users are less likely to buy if they are presented with just one option. They will be left unsatisfied with their consumer experience, itching for more options, and searching for better alternatives that might be out there waiting. Buyers like to have choices.

This is also true when you provide a colleague with feedforward information. If you provide him with multiple ways to behave more effectively, your colleague's likelihood of choosing one of the solutions is significantly greater.

Sammi, a former client of mine, wanted to provide Michelle, a co-worker, with some feedforward information on better ways to schedule work activities on a group project. Up until that time, Michelle had either failed to schedule or double-scheduled recurring work activities, which caused confusion and frustration for other team members. Sammi met with Michelle, shared her observations and experiences, and provided three feedforward suggestions of ways Michelle could organize the workload more effectively. Michelle listened, asked a couple of questions, and happily chose one of the three options.

ACTION

Think of an issue you would like to discuss with a colleague at work. Can you come up with three feedforward suggestions you could offer her as ways to resolve the issue?

In my bravery survey, seventy-five percent of participants said they would have been braver at work if their colleagues had seemed more flexible when they shared ideas. If you provide your colleague with more than one option, the likelihood of his listening and discussing those options, as well as coming up with options of his own, is far greater. After all, everyone wants to get better at his job and make advancements in his career. And being flexible enough to share and discuss multiple solutions to a problem, regardless of who comes up with the ideas, is a great way for your colleague to make those kinds of progress.

Notice that in the story above, Sammi gave Michelle three ideas to consider. Why the magic number three? Let's take a look at a principle called the Rule of Three.

The Rule of Three

Harappa is an Indian-based learning and development organization that published an article entitled, "How to Communicate Better with the Rule of Three."[4] In it, they use the Rule of Three as a writing principle that suggests that a trio of events or characters is more humorous, satisfying, or effective than other numbers. In addition, they show that a list of three entities combines both brevity and rhythm and has the smallest amount of information necessary to create a pattern that you can remember.

The Rule of Three is not exclusive to the Harappa article but is found everywhere in our world's cultures. Here are some examples of its application that might be familiar to you:

- Beginning, middle, end—the parts of a story
- Red, yellow, green—the colors on a stoplight
- Snap! Crackle! Pop!—the slogan for a breakfast cereal
- Aramis, Athos, and Porthos—the Three Musketeers (Bibliophiles know there are actually Four Musketeers—don't forget D'Artagnan— yet Alexander Dumas didn't name his book *The Four Musketeers.* Perhaps he was an early adopter of the Rule of Three!)
- Larry, Moe, and Curly—the Three Stooges
- See no evil, speak no evil, hear no evil—the three wise monkeys
- Stop, drop, and roll—a fire safety slogan
- Life, liberty, and the pursuit of happiness—rights outlined in the Declaration of Independence
- The ghosts of Christmas past, present, and future—spirits who visit Ebenezer Scrooge in Charles Dickens's *The Christmas Carol*

The list goes on and on and on. (Wink wink!)

So, the next time you are being brave with a colleague and offer her suggestions of ways she could be more effective, show your flexibility by providing her with not one but three options, thus avoiding the insinuation that there is only one correct solution. Presenting her with three possible solutions allows her to select the choice she feels most comfortable implementing. As we've shown, when a person is presented with choices, her likelihood of participating in the solution is far greater.

The ability to come up with multiple ideas, evaluate each of them, and then select the most effective option requires something mental health professionals call cognitive flexibility, another useful tool for being brave at work.

The Importance of Cognitive Flexibility

Cognitive flexibility refers to the ability to mentally switch between two or more ideas or to think about multiple ideas simultaneously.[5] Amit, who was mentioned at the start of this chapter, did not possess cognitive flexibility. He was unable to process more than one idea at a time and typically the idea he focused on was his own. Most of us, however, when respectfully and professionally presented with a series of new thoughts or ideas, can effectively evaluate each of them and determine which one is the best choice for us. Being cognitively flexible while listening to and thinking about new ideas is necessary for us to help ourselves, our teams, and our organization.

The importance of cognitive flexibility is characterized in an article published on The Conversation website entitled "IQ Tests Can Measure It, But Cognitive Flexibility is Key to Learning and Creativity," by Barbara Sahakian, Christelle Langley, and Victoria Leong. In the article, the authors state, "Cognitive flexible thinking is key to creativity—in other words, the ability to think of new ideas, make novel connections between ideas, and make new inventions. It also supports academic and work skills such as problem-solving."[6] Simply stated, cognitive flexibility refers to being open to new ideas.

The Flexibility Component

When you are preparing to have a brave discussion with a colleague, you can first work with a co-worker to practice the words you are going to use to motivate your colleague to discuss the topics you want to discuss (practice), then decide the best way to share what you and others are experiencing (presence), and then determine how to provide appropriate feedforward to your colleague (future-focus). Once you've worked out those elements of the TBT Model©, it's time to concentrate on the last part: flexibility.

This is a detailed look at ways to include flexibility in your brave-at-work discussions.

Be Open to Giving and Receiving New Ideas and Solutions

This is where you will have to put in some hard work as you need to be prepared to discuss three ways (employing the Rule of Three) for your colleague to say or do things differently that will help him be more effective. There are many ways for you to come up with new and fresh ideas:

- **Your own past experiences:** Perhaps you have seen similar issues in the past and have thoughts on how to make positive progress in new ways.

- **The experiences of others:** Maybe your conversation coach or a leader or mentor may have ideas on how to do things differently to be more effective.

- **Google it:** Remember that technology now provides unlimited access to articles, experiments, and experiences from thousands of others on your topic of interest.

- **Ask your colleague:** During your conversation, remember to ask your colleague for his ideas about ways he can be more effective at work. After all, he is the one most impacted by any changes being made and he is the one who will implement them.

Help Your Colleague Identify a Path to Improvement

Selecting a new way to be more effective may be difficult for your colleague and might require some assistance from you. But first, take a moment to remember how hard you thought it would be to have that discussion with your colleague. Great job getting this far!

As you work to conclude the conversation, here are three methods you can use to help your colleague identify the best step he can take to make positive progress:

- **Prioritize ideas:** Working with your colleague, prioritize your ideas based on their ease of execution and scope of impact. The easier-to-implement ideas that have the broadest impact should be at the top of the list.

- **Pilot ideas to see if they work:** You can't use a crystal ball to determine whether or not your ideas will work. So, based on your prioritized list, suggest that your colleague select one option and try it out. After a specified period of time, evaluate its effectiveness. If the solution is working—great! If not, encourage your colleague to pilot the second option on the prioritized list.

- **Remember that time has an impact on ideas:** Your selected idea may work at first but then become less effective. As time passes, new or modified ideas may need to be implemented to keep up with changes within your organization. Schedule a meeting with your colleague several months or even a year after your initial conversation to assess progress and determine if newer ideas are needed.

Offer or Accept an Appropriate Apology

Occasions may arise where you or your colleague need to apologize for behavior that others may not have experienced well. In his book, *Effective Apology: Mending Fences, Building Bridges, and Restoring Trust*, renowned author, speaker, and consultant John Kador shares this recipe for an effective apology: "We apologize when we accept responsibility for an offense or grievance and express remorse in a direct, personal, and unambiguous manner, offering restitution and promising not to do it again."[7] Apologizing—admitting that you did something wrong—takes a great deal of flexibility.

Apologizing is neither easy nor common as most of us find apologizing difficult to do. In Guy Winch's article, "We all know people who can't apologize—well, here's why," he provides two reasons why apologizing is so difficult for people. "To be clear, even the most conscientious among us occasionally fails to apologize. When this happens, it's usually for one of two reasons: (1) We don't care enough about the other person or the relationship to take on the emotional discomfort of owning our mistake and apologizing for it; or (2) We believe our apology won't matter."[8] If you believe you need to apologize for a past interaction, include this thought in your talking points to ensure you say it.

Being flexible is all about listening, demonstrating curiosity, and recognizing that while you may have solutions to move forward, you might not have the best one. Considering multiple ideas and then picking the one that works best for your colleague and the organization is the best way to make positive progress.

By this point in the book, you have read how practice, presence, future-focus, and flexibility all play key roles in saying something that is hard to say or difficult for your colleague to hear. In the next chapter, we will examine brief case studies of four clients who successfully implemented each of the TBT Model© steps.

CHAPTER NOTES

[1] https://www.amazon.com/Brave-Talk-Building-Resilient-Relationships/dp/1506462448/ref=sr_1_1?crid=VXQM4Z3RV8HF&keywords=brave+talk+melody&qid=1683306837&sprefix=brave+talk+melody,aps,87&sr=8-1

[2] https://www.amazon.com/Whack-Side-Head-More-Creative/dp/0446404667/ref=sr_1_1?hvadid=598726197542&hvdev=c&hvlocphy=9002018&hvnetw=g&hvqmt=e&hvrand=5670959634499397022&hvtargid=kwd-58044506&hydadcr=15552_13558506&keywords=a+whack+on+the+side+of+the+head&qid=1690409407&sr=8-1

[3] https://www.acrwebsite.org/volumes/1015590/volumes/v41/NA-41

[4] https://harappa.education/harappa-diaries/the-rule-of-three/

[5] https://www.sciencedirect.com/topics/neuroscience/cognitive-flexibility

[6] https://theconversation.com/iq-tests-cant-measure-it-but-cognitive-flexibility-is-key-to-learning-and-creativity-163284

[7] https://www.amazon.com/Effective-Apology-Mending-Building-Restoring-ebook/dp/B005X0OLR0/ref=sr_1_1?crid=2I9EYX97QOB0N&keywords=effective+apology&qid=1679345203&sprefix=effective+apology,aps,153&sr=8-1

[8] https://ideas.ted.com/why-some-people-cant-apologize/

QUOTES
from the Bravery Survey

"I did not defend myself and said nothing to a leader, which resulted in his bad behavior repeating itself."

. . .

"I avoided having a tough conversation with a colleague and I know it would have been better to have had it."

. . .

"I was not brave at work and the desired outcomes were simply mediocre."

. . .

"I was not brave at work by not addressing a co-worker who was not treating his colleagues with respect."

. . .

"I allowed certain bad behaviors to continue so that when I did need to address it, it was a much larger problem to fix."

. . .

"I was reprimanded by a senior leader, and I wish I had the presence of mind to pause, ask clarifying questions, and solve the problem. Instead, I did nothing."

CHAPTER NINE

Using The Bravery Trick Model©

"Take a step in a direction that might feel uncomfortable—that is in itself a move that starts a change in a behavior pattern that can be pretty transformative."

– Linda Rossetti, *Expert on Organizational and Personal Transformation, Author and* Be Brave at Work© *Podcast Guest – Episode 252*

During my years as a leadership coach, I have worked with hundreds of clients and most of them have felt they needed to say something hard for them to say or difficult for their colleagues to hear. However, they avoided these potential confrontations due to fear of a negative response, nervousness about career-impacting repercussions, or lack of conversational experience. When discussing these challenging conversations with me, my clients acknowledged that they needed to demonstrate more bravery to conduct these difficult conversations with their colleagues.

Not all of my clients were ready to take this next step. But most of them chose to move forward and demonstrate bravery in the workplace, regardless of the outcome. They felt confident that if they properly prepared for the conversations, their likelihood of success was worth the investment of time, effort, sweaty hands, and fast-beating hearts. Here are four examples of clients who successfully employed the TBT Model©.

Be Brave at Work with Practice

Alyce was a partner at a successful law firm, where she was responsible for employee relations and leadership development. There were six managers at the firm who were supposed to handle problematic employees but instead, they looked the other way and left Alyce to deal with all the employee performance issues. This caused her a lot of stress and took up too much of her time. Finally, Alyce had had enough of the managers avoiding their responsibilities and decided to speak with them as a group, feeling it would be more effective to have one conversation with six leaders rather than six independent conversations.

Alyce worried about the upcoming meeting. She was fearful that she would come across as just another talking head and that everyone would nod in agreement, and leave the meeting, but change nothing. Alyce knew she had to find a way to speak with the managers that was supportive and educational, not belittling or filled with negative emotion. She needed them to accept their responsibilities to solve employee performance issues because otherwise, those problems would continue to be her problems.

To prepare for the meeting, Alyce explored the first step of the TBT Model©: practice. Here is what she did.

- **Collected her thoughts on paper:** Employee performance management and employee relations are complex issues with many moving pieces, so Alyce knew she needed to be clear in her communication of these topics during the meeting or else everyone would get lost in the details. To organize her thoughts, Alyce found it very helpful to dump all of the data from her head onto paper and then sort it by topic.

- **Drafted an opening:** Alyce knew that the beginning of the meeting would set the tone for the entire conversation, so she created an opening that was visionary, energizing, and inspiring. In it, she welcomed the managers, thanked them for coming, and explained why she had asked them to meet with her.

- **Described the impact:** Next, Alyce wrote notes clearly explaining to the managers the impact their underperformance was having on her, their colleagues, and the organization. She avoided negativity by stating real-life examples to which the listeners could relate.

- **Provided motivation:** Alyce then flipped her presentation and focused on the benefits enhanced leadership by the managers would provide each of them, the employees, and the organization. In her notes, she included topics full of vision, energy, and inspiration to motivate the managers to change.

- **Created a list of next steps:** Although Alyce planned for the managers to create their own list of next steps toward improvement during the meeting, she also drafted a list in case they needed help to expand their thinking. These next steps described what each manager could do to help solve the employee performance problems.

- **Converted her thoughts to talking points:** Alyce recognized that the managers had a limited amount of time to discuss the issue, so she created a short PowerPoint presentation that listed her talking points for the meeting's opening, impact, motivation, and next steps. With that as a visual agenda, the meeting was less likely to get sidetracked by unimportant details.

- **Found a colleague with whom she practiced:** Alyce wanted to practice the delivery of her thoughts so when she met with her managers it would not be the first time she presented this important information. She also wanted to check with someone else to make sure her information made sense, she had avoided any hot-button topics, and her talking points would motivate her managers to be actionable. She enlisted a colleague at another law firm to be her conversation coach, ensuring that this friend would keep the information confidential. Alyce practiced her conversation with her coach several times, adjusting her presentation based on her friend's valuable advice.

In preparing for her meeting with the six managers, Alyce found the most helpful portion of the practice step of the TBT Model© was getting all of her thoughts out of her head and onto paper. She believed this helped her to obtain clarity on the main issues so that she could create a focused presentation to motivate the managers. Alyce also felt that this step helped reduce much of the fear that had prevented her from speaking with her colleagues about the problem earlier.

When I spoke with Alyce again a few months after she met with the managers, she trumpeted the positive impact her discussion had had on her company. While she felt the managers still had a long way to go to fully handle the employee performance issues at the firm, she believed she had successfully and positively discussed the problem with them—a true moment of bravery at work for her.

ACTION
Identify ways practicing a difficult discussion with a colleague would help you feel braver.

Be Brave at Work with Presence

Richard was a vice president of technology at an online services organization. For several months, he avoided a conversation he knew he needed to have with Henry, a direct report of his who was consistently late on his deliverables. Finally, matters came to a head when Richard's boss asked about Henry's capabilities due to some negative customer comments. Richard told his boss, "Henry is a valuable employee, but he's way too detail-oriented and can never leave anything alone. Also, he becomes very frenetic when he is stressed or has a lot of work to do."

Since his boss was now aware of the issues, Richard knew he had to have a conversation with Henry before things got worse. However, Richard was afraid that if he pushed too hard on the topic, Henry might quit his job altogether, an undesirable result. Richard decided that a good way to ensure a productive conversation with Henry—especially since Henry often overreacted when stressed—was to follow step two of the TBT Model©: presence. Richard believed that being attuned to and able to express his true thoughts, feelings, and values, respectfully and professionally to Henry, would help him share what he and others were experiencing with Henry's behavior at work.

In anticipation of their meeting, Richard thought about both operational and strategic presence. Richard made a lot of decisions about operational presence before his conversation with Henry.

- **Location:** Richard decided to invite Henry to the cafeteria. Although this was an open area, he thought the conversation would be more palatable in an open public setting rather than a closed-in private office or conference room.

- **Seating:** Richard planned to sit on the same side of the table as Henry, to ensure good eye contact, equity of power, and connection. Richard hoped this would reassure Henry that he wanted him to succeed.

- **Time of day:** Richard felt it would be good to talk with Henry near the end of the day when a lot had been accomplished, versus the start of the day when there was still much work to do and Henry might be feeling pressured.

- **Avoiding distractions:** The cafeteria would also provide a meeting place where phones and computers would not distract them from their conversation and, as it was near the end of the day and the cafeteria would be largely empty, interruptions from other employees would be minimal.

Richard knew he would have to be fully present with Henry to effectively accomplish his goals for their conversation. Before their meeting, he committed to taking several steps to increase his strategic presence, too.

- **Demonstrate curiosity:** Richard planned to share his concerns with Henry during their meeting, but he also intended to show him that he was curious about Henry's view of the situation. Richard planned to ask Henry questions such as, "What are your reasons for being late on your deliverables?" and "What benefits or repercussions are you experiencing by behaving this way?" By seeking this input from Henry, Richard showed he wanted to know Henry's perspective and he valued him as an employee.

- **Be a good listener:** Since he viewed Henry as a valuable employee, Richard planned to listen to him carefully, thinking he might learn a few things from Henry's situation that may apply to others. Richard reminded himself to lean forward, maintain positive eye contact, and reiterate some of Henry's points to physically demonstrate that he was listening.

- **Take appropriate notes:** Richard also recognized the need to take accurate notes throughout the conversation to capture words and ideas that he might need to refer to later in the meeting or at subsequent conversations with Henry.

- **Observe body language:** Richard planned to observe Henry's body language during their meeting to ensure that Henry was receptive to what was being said and was not having a negative emotional response, which could sabotage the effectiveness of their conversation. Richard understood that leaning forward, smiling, and nodding were positive body language signs whereas arms crossed over the chest, head shaking, and pulling back from the table were examples of negative body language.

- **Demonstrate empathy:** Richard knew that the best way for him to achieve positive progress with Henry was to be empathetic with him by walking in Henry's shoes and fully understanding what he was feeling and why. In this way, Richard could help Henry make progress as a colleague versus dictating change as a boss. Richard planned to use key phrases such as "I understand why you feel that way" and "I can see why you would view it that way" since they would feel supportive and helpful to Henry.

By carefully planning his operational and strategic presence for his conversation with Henry, Richard felt ideally prepared to help Henry realize the impact of his undesirable behavior and strategize ways to correct it. Richard especially appreciated the information he gained about body language and found himself referring to it in his interactions with other colleagues.

I bumped into Richard at a networking event a couple of months after he met with Henry and asked him how the conversation had gone. Richard said that it had exceeded his expectations. Being fully present with Henry, undistracted, curious, listening, and demonstrating empathy had helped both of them create an effective pathway for Henry's improvement on the job, thus making it possible for the company to retain a valuable employee. Richard was proud of himself for having that brave-at-work conversation and planned to have more in the future.

ACTION
Think about your operational and strategic presence at your next workplace meeting. What would you do to manage these factors of the conversation?

Be Brave at Work with Future-Focus

Felipe was a customer service manager at an auto components manufacturer. Although he did not supervise Genevieve, she was one of his co-workers and as such he felt an obligation to tell her about how her extreme bluntness was upsetting other employees. Genevieve reported to an off-site leader, whose office was in another state, so no one in authority was around Genevieve to observe her and help her resolve her bluntness problem. Felipe worried that unless she improved her behavior soon, the problem would grow past the point of repair.

Felipe was afraid if he spoke with Genevieve, she or others at the company might get angry and say that he was doing something better suited to her boss. And, since he was not her boss, he was worried that any attempt to provide her with feedforward information would be rejected.

Despite these possible repercussions, Felipe decided to help Genevieve by having a conversation with her about the problem, employing the TBT Model© of bravery. He practiced what he intended to say to Genevieve at the meeting and then was consciously present with her during their conversation. In addition, Felipe intentionally employed step three of the model: future-focus. By focusing on the future and providing feedforward ideas to Genevieve, he was able to avoid being stuck in the past and being perceived as someone who was attempting to manage her behavior or oversee her performance. To achieve future-focus at the meeting, Felipe took the following steps:

- **Reflect versus remember**. Felipe recognized that speaking about the past was necessary for Genevieve to put their conversation into context, but he didn't want their discussion to get so stuck in the past that talking about the future became secondary. Felipe selected three specific occurrences of Genevieve's blunt behavior and asked for her reflections on them so they could consider, meditate, and contemplate these experiences versus reliving them. This allowed them to reflect, move forward, and not get stuck in the past.

- **Focus on the future**. Felipe carefully sculpted his comments to help Genevieve focus on future behaviors she could control versus past behaviors that she could not change. Rather than saying, "don't," "stop," or "never," he said, "do," "start," or "always." Using that language made the conversation feel more positive and actionable, too. For example, saying, "Don't be as blunt with people as you usually are," would be focusing on her past behavior and wasn't actionable since Genevieve may not know how to do that. But reminding her to, "Always ensure you understand your colleague's problem before you share your perspective," was future-focused and actionable—and thus the correct way to phrase this suggestion.

- **Provide feedforward.** By utilizing feedforward versus feedback, Felipe was able to ensure that both he and Genevieve had a positive meeting experience because feedforward promotes the following outcomes:

  - **Generates ideas that could change the future.** Feedforward helped Genevieve envision and focus on a positive future, not a failed past.

  - **Helps Genevieve learn to improve:** Feedforward was a positive experience that assisted Genevieve in focusing on solutions, not problems.

  - **Avoids the feeling of being criticized:** Genevieve did not perceive feedforward as a personal critique since it discusses something that has not yet happened.

  - **Provides faster and more efficient solutions:** When giving feedforward ideas to Genevieve, Felipe said, "Here are four ideas for the future. Please accept these in the positive spirit that they are given and ignore what doesn't make sense for you." By using this method of providing feedforward information, Felipe and Genevieve didn't waste time debating the quality of the ideas or proving their validity.

  - **Encourages Genevieve to listen more attentively:** If he had used feedback, Felipe knew that Genevieve would not fully listen since her brain would be spending too much energy composing her response. By employing feedforward, she was able to listen fully since her response was simply, "Thank you."

Before his conversation with Genevieve, Felipe had been unfamiliar with the concept of feedforward. Afterward, he found himself using it in many situations, both at work and in his personal life.

I followed up with Felipe a few weeks after his conversation with Genevieve to find that he was thrilled with the progress they had made. What Felipe thought might be a one-time meeting of the two of them had evolved into a four-part conversation. Genevieve was genuinely concerned about the negative impact her behavior might have on her career development and was eager to discuss and implement next steps to modifying her perceived bluntness. She was so appreciative of Felipe showing her some colleague-care, she had treated him to a delicious thank-you dinner.

ACTION
What could you do to stay future-focused during your next brave-at-work conversation?

Be Brave at Work with Flexibility

Abby, a manager at a temp agency, was so frustrated with her off-site boss, Rosalie, that she seriously considered quitting her job. During the year they had worked together, Abby found that Rosalie rarely answered her phone or responded to emails or text messages. If Abby or one of her colleagues needed something from Rosalie, they had to go see her face-to-face, which was difficult because they were based in different buildings a few blocks apart. These issues made it very hard for Abby and her colleagues to work with Rosalie. Since Abby was a manager at the company, many of her co-workers came to her looking for updates and answers that only Rosalie would know, adding to Abby's frustration.

She wondered if Rosalie's lack of communication was a bad habit or a deliberate part of a leadership plan. If it were part of a plan, Abby did not feel it was a very good one.

Finally, Abby resolved to discuss the issue with Rosalie and set up a meeting with her. In addition to practicing what she intended to say to Rosalie, planning to be very present during their conversation, and intending to be future-focused, Abby resolved to focus on step four of the TBT Model©: flexibility. Since Abby did not know the cause of Rosalie's behavior, she knew she would have to be flexible in their discussion of solutions. Rather than stating that she had the one and only answer to the problem, Abby needed to demonstrate cognitive flexibility. This is a list of flexibility guidelines Abby employed in her conversation with Rosalie:

- **Utilize the Rule of Three.** Abby knew that Rosalie would participate more in solving the problem if she could choose the solution, and that too few or too many suggestions would complicate the conversation. So, Abby prepared three viable solutions Rosalie could select from to make effective progress.

- **Be open to giving and considering new ideas and solutions:** Conversations are a two-way street, so the solution to the problem would not come from just Abby or just Rosalie. During their conversation, both of them needed to be open to giving and considering new ideas to ensure they would reach an effective solution.

- **Help identify a new way to have a better outcome:** Perhaps Rosalie was unaware of the effects of her uncommunicative behavior or maybe she knew hers was not an effective way to operate yet did not know how to fix the issue. In either case, she may require assistance in selecting the best solution to her communication problem. Abby realized she could assist Rosalie in these ways:

  - **Help her prioritize ideas:** During their conversation, Abby and Rosalie would discuss several different ways for Rosalie to make progress. Once the possible options were identified, they needed to be prioritized by ranking the ideas based on selection criteria, such as prioritizing the solutions that had the broadest impact, were short-term and more visible, or reflected the way Rosalie wanted to be experienced as a leader.

- **Encourage her to pilot ideas to see if they work.** Sometimes, solutions that seem great in theory don't work out as well in practice. The best way to know if an option will work is to pilot it. To do this, let your colleagues know you are working to improve yourself and you are going to pilot a strategy to see if it works. If it works, great! If it doesn't work, pilot the next one on your prioritized list. Abby planned to encourage Rosalie to pilot her strategies.

- **Remind her that time has an impact on ideas:** No idea will work forever, so after about six months, Abby needed to remind Rosalie to consult with her co-workers to see if her new strategies continued to make a difference. If they were still working, she should continue using them. If not, she should move on to a different strategy.

I bumped into Abby a couple of months after her conversation with Rosalie and she said she was thrilled that she had found the ability to be brave at work by having difficult but productive conversations that helped colleagues. Her boss, Rosalie, had been very receptive to Abby's feedforward and immediately began working to improve her response time and connections with colleagues. Because Abby had dealt with this difficulty head-on, she no longer felt like quitting and her work life had significantly improved.

ACTION
What are some ways you would utilize flexibility in your next brave-at-work meeting?

The Bravery Trick Model©

Anytime you have something to say to a colleague that might be hard for you to say or may be hard for your colleague to hear, implement the TBT Model©. Here is a quick overview of the four steps of the model: practice, presence, future-focus, and flexibility.

Practice

In the context of the TBT Model©, practice means performing recurring activities that are designed to help you get better at a skill or behavior that will motivate your colleague to discuss a topic you want to share. To be brave at work, do the following:

- Get your thoughts out of your head and onto paper
- Identify why what you are saying is important
- Motivate the listener to pay attention, listen, and consider moving forward
- List the next steps necessary to move forward
- Convert your thoughts into talking points, or reminders of what you want to ensure that you say
- Find a colleague and practice your conversation

Presence

Presence means being aware of and able to express your true thoughts, feelings, values, and potential to share what you and others are experiencing. Being brave involves being both operationally and strategically present. To ensure you are operationally present, you should do the following:

- Identify a good location for the meeting
- Figure out the optimal seating arrangement
- Select the best time of day for the conversation to take place
- Identify ways to minimize distractions

To ensure you are strategically present, do the following:

- Demonstrate curiosity

- Be an active listener
- Take notes
- Observe and integrate body language
- Demonstrate empathy

Future-Focus

Being future-focused means concentrating your energy and effort on what might be and creating the belief that your colleague needs to do some things differently to be more effective. To use future-focus to be brave at work, do the following:

- Reflect versus remember
- Focus on the future
- Provide feedforward versus feedback

Flexibility

Within the TBT Model©, flexibility means being open to giving and considering new ideas and solutions to move a situation forward in positive ways. Being flexible is necessary for both you and your colleague because both of you must professionally and respectfully create and receive new ideas. When being flexible in a brave-at-work situation, do the following:

- Utilize the Rule of Three by always having three choices of ideas to share with your colleague during conversations that require bravery
- Identify new ways to have a better outcome:
  - Prioritize ideas since not all ideas are created equal
  - Pilot the best solution to see if it actually works
  - Remember that solutions may work for a limited time and may need to be adapted or replaced to suit a changing work environment.

We have discussed how the TBT Model© can help you say things that are hard to say or may be difficult for your colleagues to hear. Yet, even the best-laid plan does not always work as we thought it would. Let's look at ways you can minimize obstacles that might occur as you are working to be brave at work.

QUOTES
from the Bravery Survey

"Not being brave at work created tremendous anxiety for me. It is so hard keeping something private and withholding it versus doing something about it."

. . .

"I was not more direct with an employee whose performance was deficient."

. . .

"A white male colleague made a comment about a difficult encounter with a female co-worker and brought in the fact, unnecessarily, that she was black. I regret that I was not brave and didn't confront him on his comments."

. . .

"Early in my career, I often recognized dissonance or negativity in others. Rather than ask them about my observations, I did not, and we spent a lot of time worrying about it and not being productive."

. . .

"I wimped out confronting a colleague who was attempting to torpedo my role. I felt powerless and insecure."

CHAPTER TEN

Minimizing Obstacles to Bravery at Work

"If I am human and harmless, others need to include me as a participant in a social exchange."

– **Timothy Clark**, *Organizational Anthropologist, Founder/CEO of the LeaderFactor, and* Be Brave at Work© *Podcast Guest* – *Episodes 54, 55, & 56*

Elton was a senior marketing manager at a financial consulting firm and is frequently not brave at work. He was afraid if he spoke his mind, his boss, Rita, might think or say something like:

"I don't care what you think."

"What you are saying is stupid."

"I am going to demote you for saying that."

"How dare you come into my office and say that?"

"Get out!"

Elton also did not feel that he knew Rita well enough to be honest with her. And he felt he was too junior to her to offer suggestions or advice. "Who am I to tell her something that might be hard for her to hear? Isn't that her boss's job?" By anticipating Rita's negative reaction, Elton was creating obstacles to being candid with her, even though he was pretty sure his suggestions would be helpful.

Obstacles to Bravery at Work and Possible Solutions

There are many reasons why you may not be brave at work. Five of the most common are these:

- Your organization does not value or recognize bravery at work
- You believe your boss or colleague will not receive the information well
- You don't think you are the right person to provide the feedback
- You don't feel skilled enough on how to be brave at work
- You work remotely and seldom see your boss or colleagues in person

Let's take a look at each of these reasons, one at a time, and consider possible ways to deal with them in a work environment.

Your Organization Does Not Value or Recognize Bravery at Work

If your organization does not support bravery at work, bravery is less likely to occur. Supporting a philosophy of bravery may be a major change for your organization and a lot of people don't like change. According to the managementisajourney.com article, "Organizational Change: 8 Reasons Why People Resist Change," these are the most common reasons:

- Loss of status or job security
- Poorly aligned (non-reinforcing) reward systems
- Surprise and fear of the unknown
- Peer pressure
- Climate of mistrust
- Organizational politics
- Fear of failure
- Faulty implementation approach[1]

If your company does not currently support brave practices, management personnel may be reluctant to initiate them because they harbor some of these fears.

ACTION

What are the reasons bravery does not exist at your place of work?

Another reason bravery may be absent from your workplace is that people tend to practice behaviors that are rewarded. Conversely, if your company does not reward bravery, you and your colleagues will not be motivated to be brave. In the article, "The Power of Rewards and Why We Seek Them Out," which was published on theconversation.com website, the authors posit, "When we get a reward, special pathways in our brain become activated. Not only does this feel good, but the activation also leads us to seek out more rewarding stimuli. This influences our likelihood that we will engage in this activity again."[2] In other words, if your organization wants bravery in the workplace, then acts of bravery must be rewarded.

If your organization doesn't support being brave at work, there are steps you can take as an individual to initiate a workplace conversation about bravery. Here are three situations that could potentially provide you with opportunities to start such a discussion:

- When you initially interview for a role at a new organization, ask about the company's stance on educating, recognizing, and rewarding bravery. This is a great way to assess the existence of bravery as a core value for the organization.
- Then, during your time there, support and promote the value placed upon workplace bravery and identify future bravery goals. But remember that a tremendous amount of time and energy will be required to convert a team or an organization from an entity that does not educate, recognize, and reward bravery to one that does. Caryn, a client of mine, created a three-year bravery integration plan for her engineering and construction firm to move behavior from a place where colleagues were overly polite to one another to a place where colleagues respectfully helped each other perform more effectively. While her organization is only about one

year into her plan, she has noticed that due to its positive influence, leaders in her company are exhibiting bravery more often by saying what needs to be said and doing what needs to be done.

- If you end up leaving an organization, your exit interview could be a great place to share your perspective on the company's level of support of bravery as a cultural behavior. In the BetterUp.com article, "What to Say During an Exit Interview: 7 Do's and Don'ts," Content Marketing Manager Elizabeth Perry writes, "Practicing integrity in the workplace means being honest at work—and when you're leaving. Exit interviews aim to help with employee retention and to better understand team dynamics. An exit interview is an opportunity to provide honest feedback, but not anything unprofessional and inappropriate. You can offer negative feedback if it's done clearly and respectfully."[3] Since you are leaving your organization, you needn't fear repercussions and your comments might make things easier for future personnel. If that organization hears negative bravery reports from enough employees, the likelihood of them doing something positive about it is greater.

One way to bolster your likelihood of personally promoting bravery at work is by building positive relationships within your company. Before you propose your brave ideas to the administration, tap into your network of colleagues at work to gain support for your innovations. As the saying goes, "You can't fight city hall," meaning it is harder for one person to challenge a bureaucracy or a process than it is for a group of people.[4] If co-workers agree and support your suggestions, your likelihood of success is far greater. When you approach co-workers to build support for your ideas, follow these steps:

- Write up a set of talking points that clearly identifies the ideas you want to propose.

- Select three to five individuals within your network who you feel would be open to considering your ideas. Try to find individuals of different administrative levels (i.e., bosses, colleagues, and direct reports) to provide a wider sampling of reactions.

- Share your ideas with these individuals, and then ask them these two follow-up questions: (1) "If I have a respectful and professorial conversation with my boss about these ideas, do you think she will listen?" and (2) "If my boss should ask your opinion about these matters, will you support me?" Remember that finding others within your organization who agree with your perspective and support your position will significantly increase your likelihood of success.

As time passes and your co-workers and boss see the success you have with this type of conversation, your organization may think differently about workplace bravery and take steps to integrate this key behavior into their vision, values, and mission, a topic we will explore in depth in the next chapter.

Don't let the lack of a culture of bravery at your workplace stop you from being brave at work. Even if your organization does not acknowledge or recognize bravery, they do want you to be honest with your colleagues and to help each other, which is one of the benefits of being brave at work.

ACTION

Think about bravery as an essential value of your organization's culture. If it exists, what are the ways it exists? If it does not exist, what are some steps you can take personally to start a conversation about promoting bravery at work?

You Believe Your Boss or Colleague Will Not Receive the Information Well

The most common obstacle to being brave at work is being afraid of your boss or colleague's reaction. In her LinkedIn article, "Why Leaders Won't Accept Feedback," Leadership Coach Dr. Wilma Slenders suggests some of the following reasons why your boss may reject your comments:

- They think they are above receiving any kind of feedback and reject it, as well as reject you.

- They believe they are incapable of ever making a mistake or needing to improve.

- They don't accept feedback because they don't see themselves in the same way as the person who is providing the feedback.[5]

At worst, perhaps you are worried that your boss will hate your idea and fire you for even suggesting a risky idea. This is an extreme reaction, yet you might believe that anything is possible.

To overcome the fear of an adverse reaction from your boss or colleague, utilize the TBT Model©: practice, presence, future-focus, and flexibility when presenting him with your proposal. However, realize that regardless of how well you present your ideas to him, his reaction may not be as positive as you'd like it to be since no behavioral model can guarantee you a 100 percent success rate. Only you know the right time, the right topic, and the right person with whom to be brave and honest.

Clint was a director of an information technology company who was having a hard time working with his boss, Zach. Zach was disorganized and often confused his co-workers. Clint liked his boss and wanted to provide him with some feedforward to help him become better organized, yet delayed doing so for months because he feared the conversation would not go well. When another valuable employee quit, naming Zach's behavior as a key motivation for her exit, Clint seized the moment and respectfully and professionally shared some ideas and thoughts to help Zach build his self-awareness. To Clint's surprise, the conversation went great—Zach welcomed his suggestions and their work environment improved.

Fearing how a boss or colleague will react to tough feedforward does not mean you should avoid being brave at work; it means that regardless of how well you deliver the information, you cannot be sure of how he will react. As Qingzhou Sun, Huanren Zhang, Jing Zhang, and Xiaoning Zhang state in their *Frontiers in Psychology* article, "Why Can't We Accurately Predict Others' Decisions?": "Individuals often fail to accurately predict others' decisions in a risk environment."[6] Assess the situation and approach your colleague at a time you feel she may be open to hearing what you have to say. If your boss or colleague listens and evolves, congratulations! Your act of bravery made a positive difference in your workplace environment. If she reacts badly and doesn't change, you received important information about your relationship with your boss. With it, you can decide what you want to do going forward, whether that be attempting another brave conversation with your boss, requesting a transfer to another department, or moving to a different company, one that values your bravery.

You Don't Feel You Are the Right Person to Provide Feedback

When you recognize the need to say something to a colleague at work that is hard for you to say or difficult for her to hear, you might rationalize that providing this feedback is not your job, especially if the colleague is not one of your direct reports. Yet, as the saying goes, "If not you, who? If not now, when?" If you see behavior from your boss or colleague that prevents her from being effective, you have an obligation to be brave at work by respectfully and professionally saying something to help her. After all, isn't this what leadership is all about? Many organizations are pursuing a "speak-up" environment. As stated in a OneTrust blog, "Why Speak-Up Culture Matters and How to Build Yours," ethics and compliance lawyer Gbemi Yusuff writes, "A speak-up environment is a workplace culture where employees feel safe sharing their ideas and concerns, reporting misconduct, and informing the company about potential ethics violations."[7] Rather than shrugging off or ignoring the responsibility of helping that co-worker, consider the impact your bravery could have.

Elton, the senior marketing manager with whom we started the chapter, decided that regardless of the leadership levels that separated him and his boss, Rita, saying something professionally and respectfully was better than not saying anything at all. So, he did it. In his conversation with Rita, he acknowledged the difference in their levels and was surprised when she dismissed it as irrelevant. It turns out Rita agreed with Elton that hearing something helpful, even from a subordinate, was a good thing. She thanked Elton for his input, and they discussed next steps toward a possible solution, thus promoting a "speak-up" culture at work.

So, rather than avoiding a thorny issue with a boss or colleague, think of a way to say something to help her. It is far better for you to be brave and say something today than have your boss or colleague come to you months later and ask, "Why didn't you say something to me when you first saw this problem? It wouldn't have been as big an issue back then as it is now." Don't avoid difficult situations at work, even if you think you are not the ideal person to confront the issue. Instead, practice, be present, focus on the future, and be flexible.

You Don't Feel Skilled Enough to Be Brave at Work

Another classic rationalization to avoid being brave is that you fear you lack the skills to deal with the issue. And yet, everyone has to start somewhere. At one time, Arnold Schwarzenegger lifted his first weight, Tiger Woods hit his first golf ball, and Hillary Clinton gave her first speech. Although I was not present for any of these seminal events, I guarantee that each of these individuals was mediocre at best the first time they did what they are famous for today. As Academy Award-winning actress Helen Hayes said, "The expert at anything was once a beginner."[8]

Veronica, a close colleague of mine, recognized her lack of skill at being brave at work and dedicated herself to practicing and building her competency to get better at it. She enlisted me as her conversation coach and practiced for her first brave workplace conversation over and over until she felt she had developed her skills enough to pull it off. You should have seen her face when she told me afterward that the meeting went well, and that she was already planning her next brave-at-work discussion with another colleague.

Just like Veronica, you will be challenged the first time you try being brave at work. Consider these tips if you feel unprepared or under-skilled:

- **Practice:** Remember that you must practice any skill or behavior before you can become good at it, even if the skill or behavior is something you love. So, if you want to bravely say something hard to say or hard for someone to hear, follow the first step of the TBT Model© and practice first.

- **Take baby steps:** Don't bite off more than you can chew by tackling a huge issue at the highest level of your organization's administration. Instead, start with a lesser topic or a colleague at a lower level of the organization and use the TBT Model© to say something that needs to be said or may be hard for them to hear. Then move up to a bigger issue at a higher administrative level. Then another. In a short time, your skill set will grow, and you will get a better sense of how to employ the model effectively.

- **Pilot:** Once you have practiced the TBT Model© on lesser issues and you feel comfortable being present, focusing on the future, and being flexible, you are ready to confront one of your main issues— something you really want to help fix within your organization. So many of my clients tell me once they've said something to a boss or colleague that they have been hesitating to say, they feel fantastic. One client told me that after months of dreading a discussion, she finally said something to her boss because she was convinced it would be helpful to her. The conversation went so well, and her boss was so deeply appreciative of her input that afterward, my client went back to her own office, closed the door, and did a cheerleader jump in celebration.

You Work Remotely and Seldom See Your Boss or Colleagues in Person

In 2021, as we edged our way through the COVID-19 pandemic, the United States Census Bureau reported that the number of Americans working from home tripled, from 9 million (5.7% of the working population) to 27.6 million (17.9%).[9] Experts in workplace planning estimate that by 2025, as many as 36.2 million Americans will be working full-time or part-time from home[10], as an increasing number of employers welcome remote workers.

If you are planning a conversation with a boss or colleague that requires bravery, an in-person meeting is always best, for many of the reasons we have discussed in this book. If you are unable to be in the same room because you work virtually, you might rationalize that it isn't possible to have an effective conversation remotely and so avoid even trying.

"Not true!" says Richard Newman, founder and CEO of BodyTalk, a global leader in evidence-based training on the psychology of communication, and a guest on the *Be Brave at Work*© podcast (Episode 258). "Virtual working has actually increased the need for people to be brave. Because we are not seeing each other in person, greater candor is needed in order to ensure you and your colleagues are moving in the right direction."[11] In other words, remote working situations may require even more brave conversations than traditional in-office positions.

Consider these tips as you demonstrate a brave moment with a colleague virtually:

- **Have your cameras on:** During your virtual conversation, turn on your computer's camera and encourage your colleague to do the same so you can see any non-verbal signals from the other person such as facial expressions, body movement and posture, and gestures. In this way, you can assess any changes in mood or attitude as you are being brave with him.

- **Be prepared:** Since virtual conversations are naturally more difficult, your colleague may get distracted by a barking dog, crying child, or unanticipated UPS delivery. In anticipation of unexpected distractions, you must be as prepared as possible, utilizing the TBT Model© to help you manage the conversation effectively.

- **Seek clarity more frequently:** When you are being brave with a coworker in person, you must frequently verify that she is clear on your observations and the reasons you are saying something that is hard to say or hard to hear. During a virtual conversation, the risks of misunderstanding are exacerbated, requiring you to pause more frequently and ensure your colleague understands what you are saying to her. If you ask for clarity and she isn't clear, restate what you have said until your colleague understands your point. Once she is clear, move forward.

Most things that are difficult to discuss are important to say. Yet, we all can rationalize why we should not say something hard to say or hard to hear. But when we avoid these conversations, we are forced to act and behave in modified ways that make work and life more complex. Why do we do this to ourselves? Instead, I urge you to adopt the TBT Model© and use it to help as many of your colleagues as you can.

In addition to overcoming the five obstacles to being brave at work we just reviewed, bravery must be visible and relevant as a key component of your organization's culture so that you and your colleagues feel motivated to invest time and energy into this important behavior. In the next chapter, we will look at how you can help ensure your organization makes bravery a core part of its everyday behavior.

CHAPTER NOTES

[1] https://managementisajourney.com/organizational-change-8-reasons-why-people-resist-change/#:~:text=Some%20resist%20change%20as%20a,some%20power%20in%20the%20organizational.

[2] https://theconversation.com/the-power-of-rewards-and-why-we-seek-them-out-62691

[3] https://www.betterup.com/blog/author/elizabeth-perry

[4] https://www.collinsdictionary.com/us/dictionary/english/fight-city-hall#:~:text=fight%20city%20hall%20in%20American,dictionary%20entry%20for%20city%20hall

[5] https://www.linkedin.com/pulse/why-leaders-wont-accept-feedback-dr-wilma-slendersmsm pcc#:~:text=This%20may%20be%20due%20to,and%20development%20is%20not%20possible.

[6] https://www.frontiersin.org/articles/10.3389/fpsyg.2018.02190/full

[7] https://www.onetrust.com/blog/speak-up-culture-101-why-speak-up-culture-matters-and-how-to-build-yours/#:~:text=Speak%2Dup%20culture%20helps%20you,%2C%20ultimately%2C%20your%20organizational%20vision.

[8] https://www.brainyquote.com/authors/helen-hayes-quotes

[9] https://www.census.gov/newsroom/press-releases/2022/people-working-from-home.html

[10] https://www.upwork.com/press/releases/upwork-study-finds-22-of-american-workforce-will-be-remote-by-2025

[11] https://bit.ly/3JSZxN7

QUOTES
from the Bravery Survey

"I was not brave with a colleague who had addiction issues and these issues ultimately led to a very serious consequence for him."

. . .

"I might have commanded more respect if I had behaved more forcibly at work."

. . .

"Early in my career, my boss made a decision not in the best interest of the group and I did not speak up at all."

. . .

"I left my job every day at 5:00 p.m. (before others had left) as I had a ninety-minute drive home and so I was not perceived as a team player. I never addressed my feelings about this with my boss."

CHAPTER ELEVEN

How to Create an Organizational Culture That Supports Being Brave

"I observed other women who were so articulate in how they spoke up, it emboldened me to be able to speak my mind."

– **Allesandra Polizzi**, *Founder and CEO,*
Verdant Consulting and Be Brave at Work©
Podcast Guest – Episode 265

The Be Respectful Company

I recently contracted with a moderate-sized pharmaceutical company that had four organizational values, one of which was "Be Respectful." To honor this principle, the senior leadership team made it a point to never disagree or argue with anyone on the team. They interpreted being respectful as always being polite, nice, and, ultimately, avoiding difficult conversations. It was common to hear comments from team members such as:

- "Why say something that would ruin someone's day?"
- "If it is hard to say, perhaps you shouldn't say it."
- "Providing feedback often comes across as being critical of someone."
- "Don't say something if it's going to hurt someone's feelings."

This lack of candor, honesty, and bravery greatly diminished the leadership team's capability and competence.

To solve this problem, the team changed the way they interacted by resolving to always be candid with one another in constructive ways.

They found the quality of their conversations increased immediately as did their sense of engagement and partnership. Over just a few months, the team members made great progress by being professionally candid and brave with one another.

Creating an Organizational Culture That Supports Bravery

For bravery to actively occur in your workplace, your organization must embrace it as a core concept. To do this, leaders must take the following steps: (1) make bravery part of the administration's vision and value statements, (2) role-model bravery, (3) help their colleagues and direct reports be brave, (4) recognize when bravery occurs on the part of others, and (5) reward employees who help a colleague become a more effective leader by being brave. As stated in the Entrepreneur's Organization blog post, "Courage is the Key to Great Leadership": "With less fear and more courage, workers take on harder projects, deal better with change, and speak up more willingly about important issues. In short, courageous workers try more, trust more, and tell more."[1] Let's look at each of these areas integral to ensuring bravery is accepted and welcomed in a workplace.

Bravery as Part of Your Organization's Vision Statement

Almost every organization—from the local convenience mart to the multi-national relief organization—drafts a vision statement to present themselves to the world. This statement tells everyone what they do, how they do it, and why they do it, and it generally includes a list of the values the organization wants to uphold and promote. Strangely enough, most companies' vision statements do not mention bravery as one of their core values. Really. Google it—you'll see. A few organizations do mention similar concepts such as courage and conviction. For example, the United States Department of the Navy's Core Value

Charter includes this statement: "Courage is the value that gives me the moral and mental strength to do what is right, with confidence and resolution, even in the face of temptation or adversity."[2] And the vision statement for the digital consulting firm of Booz Allen Hamilton states that they promote the following: "Unflinching Courage: Bring bold thinking and speak truth to power. Maintain conviction no matter the circumstances."[3] But overall, values like bravery and courage are rarely mentioned in vision statements.

Does your organization's vision statement explicitly mention values such as courage or bravery? If not, here are some steps you can take to encourage the key decision-makers in your company to revise your vision statement:

- **Think about bravery in your organization and industry:** Compile a list of ways bravery is valued in interactions between company employees and with your customers, especially as it pertains to ensuring your organization is competitive in the marketplace. Include statements like these: "We encourage our employees to bravely offer suggestions for improvements to our organization" and "We deliberately seek collaborations with clients who bravely support ethical causes."

- **Include words and phrases that resonate in your organization and industry:** In your list, include words and phrases relating to bravery that are commonly used by your organization's decision-makers and fellow employees. Here are some examples: brave at work, courageous commitment, standing up for company values, moral and ethical strength, and conviction despite adversity. The use of words and phrases such as these is a great way to build connectivity among different people on a common topic.

- **Gather a team of allies within your company:** Share your list with colleagues who share your desire for bravery at work. Then enlist their support for your conversation with your company's key decision-makers. Remember that finding others within your organization who agree with your perspective and support your position will significantly increase your likelihood of success.

- **Present your list to the key decision-makers in your organization:** Let them know that you and others feel it's important—and necessary—to include bravery as a core company value. If they accept your list and move to amend your organization's vision statement—good job! If not, you have planted the seed of a good idea that—hopefully—will germinate at a later date.

Vendana, the chief human resources officer at a growing health services company, wanted to ensure that her organization's vision statement included a list of values that accurately represented her company. She reached out to her employees and had them identify the key behaviors they felt were important, which included candor, transparency, and bravery. Vendana wanted to support these three values and encourage their development within the company. Using them as the organization's core values, she drafted a vision statement that contained statements of the company's mission, vision, values, and motto, which she then presented to her senior leadership team and the organization's board of directors. After a few weeks of revision, the vision statement was approved and she used it to establish a set of standard operational practices for the organization based on those values, with bravery being the central value.

As Vendana realized, for bravery to exist in your organization, it must be valued. One way to ensure this is to include bravery as a core value in your company's vision statement. If bravery is clearly stated as being important to your organization, acts of bravery at work are more likely to be recognized and applauded.

Provide Bravery Training

When the value of bravery is included in your organization's vision statement, the company should make a point of recognizing and supporting employees who are brave at work. But you and your colleagues might not know what it means to behave bravely in your workplace. In my bravery survey, eighty-two percent of participants believed they would have been more likely to be brave at work with specific training. Therefore, employee bravery training needs to be a key area of focus for your organization to increase the likelihood of employees being brave at work.

Does your organization offer bravery training, either in-house or online? If so, make sure you take advantage of the opportunity to learn as much as you can about being brave at work. And encourage your colleagues to do the same.

If your organization does not currently provide bravery training, here are steps you can take to promote the addition of bravery courses to your company's employee training curriculum:

- **Think about your organization:** Identify specific company interactions—either between employees or with clients—that would greatly benefit from brave behavior. Then write up a list of courses that could teach employees that behavior. Perhaps a class on the advantages of using feedforward would be helpful to those who are averse to feedback.

- **Gather a team of allies within your company:** Once again, to increase your likelihood of success, enlist the support of like-minded colleagues who will help you in your campaign for bravery training.

- **Present your list to the key leadership development decision-makers:** Using the TBT Model©, have a brave conversation with the people within your organization who are responsible for organizing leadership development education. Hopefully, they will recognize and appreciate your bravery and thus be eager to provide bravery training to other employees.

Once your organization agrees with your proposal to provide bravery training to its employees, where do you find that training? Although very few companies provide in-house training to organizations that is specifically focused on being brave at work, several external vendors, such as the ones below, offer training that includes bravery as a component:

- **TalentLMS** (www.talentlms.com): This company prides itself on delivering learning experiences that are accessible, affordable, and enjoyable. Being Brave is a program they offer to help organizational leaders deal with the fear of bravery and overcome it to improve their leadership capabilities. The program teaches participants how to be brave at work, the benefits of bravery in the workplace, and strategies to beat their fears and be brave.

- **The Courage Course** (www.thecouragecourse.org): The Courage Course provides hands-on learning, demonstrations, and techniques to overcome the fear of failure, fear of change, fear of underperformance, and fear of confrontation. Participants learn about the psychology of fear and its impact at work, school, and in life, as well as how to unleash the power of your voice through confidence, speak to anyone effectively, and be courageous in any situation.

- **Brave Trainings** (www.bravetrainings.com): Brave Trainings provides instruction focused on diversity and equity issues, topics which may be so sensitive at your workplace that you may not feel brave enough to speak up for yourself or a colleague who may feel underrepresented. They focus on giving organizations a starting point to unpack sensitive diversity topics through authentic dialogue and consistent action. Their programs include training around allyship and identifying and confronting unconscious biases.

- **Business Training Works** (www.businesstrainingworks.com): This group offers leadership training courses, including a program that focuses on courageous leadership. This program defines courage and its impact on people and organizations, discusses the impact of fear in the workplace, and, most significantly, provides a place where participants can share personal examples from their workplace where there are opportunities to leverage courage and bravery.

The bravery training offered by companies like the ones listed above comes in many different shapes and sizes, which you need to consider when choosing which would best suit the needs of your organization. Some of the course format options may include:

- Training course versus single class
- Instructor-led versus independent study
- In-person versus online
- Hands-on versus simulation
- Lectures versus mentoring/coaching
- Group training versus one-on-one
- Management-focused versus employee-focused

By providing bravery training to its employees, your organization will be demonstrating its support of bravery as a core company value and its commitment to promoting that value within the organization.

Role-Modeling Bravery as Part of Your Organization's Leadership Style

As part of establishing an organizational culture of bravery, it is imperative that employees demonstrate bravery and thus role-model it for their co-workers. As Amy Morin, editor-in-chief of VeryWell Mind, a website providing mental health advice, writes, "According to the social learning theory, people learn by watching the behavior of others. For instance, the famous Bobo doll experiment demonstrated how kids imitate adult behavior. Researchers discovered that children treated a doll the same way the adults did. Children who watched an adult become aggressive with the doll became aggressive in their interactions as well. Meanwhile, children who watched adults treat the doll kindly imitated the kindness."[4] To put this in the context of bravery in the workplace, an effective way to encourage bravery in your organization is to role-model bravery so that others can observe your behavior and then imitate it by acting bravely themselves. Thus, an environment of bravery will be fostered within your organization.

While anyone can role-model bravery at work, the best place to start is with the leaders of your organization. According to MindTools. com, a website dedicated to advancing career professionals, "Good role models demonstrate their commitment to their employer's desired ways of working and guide the behavior of their team members accordingly."[5] Company leaders and managers need to demonstrate visible acts of bravery as frequently as possible. Employees will see them as role models and emulate their behavior.

No matter what your position is within your organization, though, you can make a big impact on your colleagues by role-modeling bravery. If you are wondering about how to effectively do this, consider these tips:

- **Look for genuine moments at work when you can respond bravely:** For example, is there something you could have said that you didn't? Analyze your interactions with others to find more of these opportunities for bravery—and then use them as role-modeling moments.

- **When you have a bravery moment or see someone else role-modeling bravery, point it out to others:** Draw attention to these brave behaviors because they demonstrate your commitment to one of your organization's core values.

- **Identify ways you can integrate bravery into your leadership style:** If you have a personal leadership style statement, make sure it includes a reference to bravery. If you don't, consider other ways to remind yourself that visibly demonstrating bravery is something you must do regularly, so your colleagues realize it is valued and encouraged by you and your organization.

Bravery Recognition

To encourage a desired behavior to grow and evolve within an organization, especially a behavior like bravery that includes interactions that may be hard to do or hear, examples of this behavior must be recognized and celebrated. According to Kelly Wong, a senior content marketing manager at Achievers.com, "One of the most obvious spiral effects of frequent employee appreciation is its ability to help reinforce the company's core values and key behaviors needed to drive business success. There is scientific evidence behind the notion that 'what gets recognized, gets repeated.' According to the Achievers' *Engagement and Retention Report*, ninety-two percent of employees agree when they're recognized for a specific action, they're more likely to take that action again in the future."[6] Recognizing workplace acts of bravery is crucial to ensuring they will continue to occur.

Many organizations have a positive attitude about bravery, yet these same organizations do not always actively recognize moments of bravery when they occur. This is the difference between *attitude* and *behavior*. According to Encyclopedia.com, "Attitude is a feeling, belief, or opinion of approval or disapproval towards something. Behavior is an action or reaction that occurs in response to an event or internal stimuli."[7] Along these same lines, when I work with clients, I often point out the difference between *ideas* (attitude) and *action* (behavior). The goal of leadership is to move from the idea of promoting bravery—"What a great moment of bravery!"—to an action that celebrates bravery— "We publicly recognize you for your bravery,"—because, as Ms. Wong points out above, recognition causes repetition.

How can you and your organization recognize acts of bravery to build a culture of bravery in your organization? Consider these tips:

- **Find ways to share examples of your bravery at work so you inspire this behavior in others:** Do you have weekly or quarterly team meetings? Does your organization have an online newsletter or some other vehicle to report and applaud moments of bravery? Use these opportunities to tell how your acts of bravery benefited you and others in your organization. When your colleagues see how your bravery is recognized, they will try to be brave, too, so they receive similar recognition.

- **Publicly share examples of your colleagues' bravery moments, too:** It's not just up to you! Your organization needs to share the account of as many moments of bravery as possible from as many employees as possible. For bravery to be an active part of your organization's culture, it needs to be practiced often by many different people.

- **Recognize bravery consistently:** Nothing will stop a desired behavior faster than an organization celebrating it at first but then ceasing to recognize it at all. This lack of recognition will signal that being brave at work is not actually important in the long run and hence, not worth the effort.

- **Establish an accountability process to ensure continued recognition:** If your company's managers are required to submit a weekly report of brave-at-work moments, they will encourage them, look for them, and report them. An accountability process is a great way to recognize and share moments of bravery.

Bravery Reward

People love being rewarded and will change their behavior to seek a reward. Over the years, several scientists conducted research that supported this social exchange theory: G.C. Homans (1958), E.J. Lawler and S.R. Thye (1999), and J.W. Thibaut and H.H. Kelley (1959). A 2008 article in the online neuroscience magazine *Neuron* summarized the scientists' results by saying they demonstrate that "an individual engages in a certain social behavior (e.g., helping others) only when the benefits of doing so outweigh the costs." Therefore, an organization must make it worth the effort for employees to demonstrate bravery. The *Neuron* article also says, "The benefits in such a case take the form not only of material rewards, such as food and money, but also of more abstract rewards, such as social approval from others."[8] In other words, bravery at work can be rewarded with extrinsic or intrinsic rewards.

- **Extrinsic rewards:** These are external rewards an employee might receive for being brave at work such as a gift card, a one-time bonus, or a pay increase. This type of reward serves as a concrete, tangible sign that bravery is valued by the organization.

- **Intrinsic rewards:** These are developmental or psychological rewards that an employee might receive such as receiving an Employee of the Month designation, being assigned a special parking space, or being promoted.

A reward for bravery—either extrinsic or intrinsic—will significantly increase the likelihood that the award winner will be brave again and that others will be brave, too, in the hope of earning a reward themselves.

To reward moments of bravery at your organization, consider using these tips:

- **Identify a way to reward employees for any type of performance or behavioral progress:** As discussed above, people will change their behavior to earn a reward, so a reward system is a great way to inspire your colleagues to model desired organizational behaviors.

- **Ensure that one aspect of your company's rewards program specifically identifies workplace bravery:** By doing so, you will be actively working to recognize positive brave behaviors that support your organization's vision and values.

- **Provide funding to promote these rewards:** Too often, great ideas are stalemated because funding was not provided for them. Having money specifically targeted for a rewards program makes it possible to consistently provide rewards for brave behavior.

Creating an organization that supports being brave may be challenging and will take some time. The language of your organization's mission and value statements must reference the importance of bravery. Your company must provide training to create a consistent application of the values of bravery. All employees, including long-term leaders and new employees, must seek out opportunities to role-model bravery and when moments of bravery occur that can be shared with others, your colleagues must be sure to let others know about them. Compelling examples of bravery at work must be recognized publicly and rewarded generously if you expect bravery moments—that will greatly benefit the organization—to happen again, and again, and again.

CHAPTER NOTES

[1] https://www.eonetwork.org/octane-magazine/special-features/courageisthekeytogreatleadership#:~:text=With%20less%20fear%20and%20more,of%20people%E2%80%94%20to%20encourage%20them.

[2] https://www.secnav.navy.mil/ethics/pages/corevaluescharter.aspx#:~:text=As%20in%20our%20past%2C%20we,continue%20to%20guide%20us%20today.

[3] https://www.boozallen.com/about/our-values-and-ethics/leading-with-purpose-and-values.html#unflinchingcourage

[4] https://bit.ly/3FC7CmU

[5] https://www.mindtools.com/a7y1ja8/how-to-be-a-good-role-model

[6] https://www.achievers.com/blog/the-positive-spiral-of-frequent-employee-appreciation/

[7] https://bit.ly/3Tt6988

[8] https://bit.ly/40jwKHc

CHAPTER TWELVE

Be Brave at Work

"The only person preventing you from choosing ways to be brave at work looks at you every day in the mirror."

– **Ed Evarts**, *your author*

I am not suggesting that being brave at work is as easy as simply following the four-step model I have presented to you. No model or method will prevent your stomach from tightening, your heart from racing, and your body temperature from rising at times when you need to be brave. If there were such a method, we would all use it to be brave all of the time. The **TBT Model**© simply provides you with suggested guidelines to help you learn to be brave, one step at a time.

You must **practice** being brave at work. In this case, practice means participating in recurring activities designed to help you improve a bravery skill or behavior and motivate your colleague to discuss the topic you want to share. Every expert had to start somewhere, and the same is true for you. If you want to be brave at work, practice can get you there. And the more you are brave, the better you will get at being brave in the future.

To be brave, you must be **present** when you are speaking with a colleague at work. Presence refers to the state of being attuned to and able to comfortably express your true thoughts, feelings, values, and potential, and to share what you and others are experiencing. Presence requires conscious attention to your and your colleague's mindset and behavior, which can connect you deeply and meaningfully.

When you are being brave, you must also **focus on the future**. By concentrating on the future, you focus your energy and effort on what might be and foster the belief that your colleague needs to do some things differently to be more effective. While most of us find it easier to reflect on the past, true bravery lies in focusing on what your colleague can do differently in the future to make a positive difference.

And finally, to create a positive outcome when being brave with a colleague, you must be **flexible** in your discussion of options. When you are flexible, you are open to giving and receiving new ideas and solutions to move a situation forward in positive ways. Realize that you don't always have the one right and true answer. Many roads can take you from one place to another and you need to be flexible with your colleagues to find the one that most effectively gets you all to your destination.

What conversations are you avoiding with your co-workers? What work relationships do you find drifting further and further apart? Are there important things you need to say to another colleague, yet never do? The TBT Model© is an effective strategy that you can use to make positive progress toward addressing these issues by being brave at work.

Take Action Now

Remember that just as Rome wasn't built in a day, you don't have to fix all of your bravery issues at once. Start small and then build up gradually to tackle larger problems. To begin, concentrate on just one issue in this way:

1. Select **one person** in your organization with whom you'd like to have a better relationship or for whom you want to provide helpful feedforward. Realize that this will involve the need for you to say something hard to say or difficult for your colleague to hear.
2. Contact your colleague and schedule a meeting with her. Schedule it enough in advance to give yourself adequate time to get ready for it.
3. Using the **TBT Model©**, carefully prepare for the conversation with your colleague.
4. Do it!

And then continue being brave. Figure out your brave conversation, plan for it, and do it. Then the next. Then the next. The TBT Model© is a simple yet effective tool you can use to make progress toward becoming brave at work. Before you know it, you will have demonstrated increased bravery, your colleagues will recognize that your help was invaluable to their growth and development, and your value will grow within your organization.

Be Brave at Work Survey Results

Conducted - 9/1/21 through 11/30/21

106 Participants

Question 1: *Can you recall any moments where you could have been braver at work, by saying something that needed to be said or doing something that needed to be done, yet you did not take action?*

Answer	# of responses	% of responses
Yes	102	96.23
No	4	3.77
Total responses	106	

Question 2: *Thinking about those moments when you could have been braver at work, which of these choices best describes your reason for not being so?*

Answer	# of responses	% of responses
Physical or emotional fear	2	1.90
Afraid of the negative impact on my role and/or job	41	39.05
Fear of the conversation converting to an argument or a difference of opinion	13	12.38
Lack of preparation	4	3.81
Lack of experience	6	5.71
Lack of training	2	1.90
Lack of certainty of a desired outcome	11	10.48
Fear of negatively impacting relational energy (the energy associated with interpersonal interactions)	26	24.76
Total responses	105	

Question 3: *If you had practiced what you wanted to say or do, would you have been more likely to be brave at work?*

Answer	# of responses	% of responses
Yes	86	82.69
No	18	17.31
Total responses	104	

Question 4: *If you had more experience saying what you wanted to say or doing what you wanted to do, would you have been more likely to be brave at work?*

Answer	# of responses	% of responses
Yes	83	79.05
No	22	20.95
Total responses	105	

Question 5: *If you had specific training on how to say what you wanted to say or do what you wanted to do, would you have been more likely to be brave at work?*

Answer	# of responses	% of responses
Yes	86	81.90
No	19	18.10
Total responses	105	

Question 6: *If you were clear on the desired outcome for what you wanted to say or do, would you have been more likely to be brave at work?*

Answer	# of responses	% of responses
Yes	84	80.00
No	21	20.00
Total responses	105	

Question 7: *If you demonstrated flexibility in the options that your colleague might take to improve his/her behavior, would you have been more likely to be brave at work?*

Answer	# of responses	% of responses
Yes	77	74.76
No	26	25.24
Total responses	105	

Question 8: *Have you ever attended a workshop or a seminar on how to demonstrate greater bravery in life or at work?*

Answer	# of responses	% of responses
Yes	24	22.64
No	82	77.36
Total responses	106	

Question 9: *Did you ever attend a class in junior high school, high school, or college on how to demonstrate greater bravery in life or at work?*

Answer	# of responses	% of responses
Yes	73	68.87
No	33	31.13
Total responses	106	

Question 10: *Upon reflection, do you ever feel regretful about missed opportunities to be brave at work with a colleague?*

Answer	# of responses	% of responses
Yes	8	7.55
No	98	92.45
Total responses	106	

Question 11: *Recalling one specific incident at work that you regret not being braver, which of these choices best describes your reason for feeling regretful?*

Answer	# of responses	% of responses
The incident caused a loss in my self-confidence	23	24.47
I fear that this incident will never leave my memory	7	7.45
I am afraid my lack of bravery may have encouraged a colleague's bad behavior, promoted someone's poor leadership style, or damaged my organization's culture	64	68.09
Total responses	106	

Question 12: *When you think about being brave at work, which of these observations best describes your assessment?*

Answer	# of responses	% of responses
Bravery is impossible in my work environment	2	1.90
I am significantly under-skilled at being brave at work	15	14.29
Being brave is frustrating and difficult to do	57	54.29
Being brave is comfortable and easy to do	31	29.52
Total responses	105	

Acknowledgments

I made a conscious decision to involve as many people as possible in the writing of *The Bravery Trick* to ensure the inclusion of a wonderful variety of voices, thoughts, opinions, and ideas. And now I offer my sincere gratitude to the following for their invaluable assistance:

- My 255+ Be Brave at Work© podcast guests—some of whom were on the podcast more than once—for generously sharing their wisdom and experiences with me and my listeners. Speaking with them enabled me to identify the need for us to be brave at work to help others and avoid future regrets—the genesis of The Bravery Trick. Thank you for your creative insights and observations, many of which appear as quotes throughout the pages of this book.

- My 106 bravery survey respondents validated many of my assumptions regarding bravery and also shared the heartfelt bravery-at-work stories that appear at the beginning of each chapter. Thank you to the participants for your candor and honesty.

- The clients and colleagues who I have had the privilege of working with over the years. Thanks for inspiring my moments of bravery and for forgiving me for the times when I missed the opportunity to be more helpful; I promise to be braver in the future!

- Lynne Heinzmann, my editor, who diligently worked with me to create the book you hold in your hands today. Somehow, she managed to read my mind and help me get my thoughts on paper. Thanks for your dedication to making this book the best it could be.

- Bob Lanphear, my book designer, who worked patiently and tirelessly to create the book cover and the layout for The Bravery Trick.

And, most importantly, my wife, Kathy, and my daughters, Sara and Caroline. Your bravery, love, and support are a constant source of inspiration for me. I could not have written this book without you.

About the Author

Ed Evarts is the founder and president of Excellius Leadership Development, an organization focused on helping clients build awareness of how others experience them in the workplace so they can manage that experience effectively.

Ed is the author of two other books: *Drive Your Career: 9 High-Impact Ways to Take Responsibility for Your Own Success* and *Raise Your Visibility & Value: Uncover the Lost Art of Connecting on the Job*. He is also the host of a bi-weekly podcast, *Be Brave at Work©*, where he chats with everyday folks and thought leaders on how to say what may be hard to say or difficult for colleagues to hear. *Be Brave at Work©* is available on Google, Apple, and Spotify.

Known for his business acumen, his ability to resolve complex human relations issues, and his enthusiastic, accessible, and responsive style, Ed skillfully builds awareness, creates action, and delivers results.

You can reach Ed in one of the following ways:
Email: ed@excellius.com
Phone/Text: (617) 549-1391
Website: www.excellius.com

Made in the USA
Middletown, DE
23 September 2024

61321984R00091